This book is dedicated to my darling brother and sister, who suffered from the same abuse as I did. I found my voice and a way forward, you both had a different journey. It fills me with deep sadness to think of what could have been and never was. You are both in a better place and I know my words also reflect your thoughts and experiences.

FROM VICTIM TO VICTOR

NARCISSISM SURVIVAL GUIDE

Dr. Mariette Jansen

Published in 2020 Indie Publishing

Copyright @2020 by Dr Mariette Jansen

All rights are reserved. No part of this publication may be reproduced, stored in a retrieval system or transmitted in any form or by any means, electronic, mechanical, photocopying, recording or otherwise, without the prior written permission of the copyright owner.

Cover design: Rocko Spigolon

Printed by Biddles Books Limited, King's Lynn, Norfolk

Endorsements

If you have a narcissist in your life, this book is for you. You will move from being a victim to victor by understanding how they operate and strategies to move away from their mind-messing power. If you are not sure if you have one in your life, this book is for you and will give you a crystal-clear answer. – Michelle Watson

This book was a revelation. I have met many people who have a rather strange outlook on life (and here I am being kind) and having read Mariette's comprehensive description of narcissism and narcissistic traits, I now understand what the issues were. I am grateful for the knowledge. – Valerie McBride Munro.

If you are not sure about it, this book is for you. From Victim to Victor has enabled me to work out a step by step plan to help break the chains from my narcissist once and for all. The helpful hints and tips have been a godsend during an incredibly dark period in my life. Thank you, Mariette, for sharing your insight and helping me to realise that I am not alone. – Charlie Witherspoon

Dutch people have a reputation for honesty and warmth and Mariette's writing confirms that. This book will help many people to find their self- belief, self-esteem and true self as they evolve from victim to victory. It seems appropriate that this book will 'emerge' at the same time roughly as society does, coming out of the Covid-19 crisis. – Linda Sewell

I always thought something was awry! But never had any real idea as to what was wrong………. with me. A random conversation with a friend made me think and helped me realise, that perhaps the problem wasn't mine to own. That's when I started to identify with what the issue was and I learnt that I have two narcissists in my life. Victim to Victor has helped me transform my thinking and built my confidence as well as given me a huge amount of guidance on how I now deal and respond to these two unfortunate souls. - A Wilkinson

Mariette's knowledge of narcissism helped me to gain the clarity and understanding I so desperately needed. The examples of techniques adopted by narcissists resonated deeply, and I was able to view my so called 'romantic relationship' through a completely new lens whilst finding a sense of self-compassion as to why and how certain patterns of behaviour continued to play out. I managed to accept that I was in a psychologically abusive relationship for over 4 years. Thanks to what I learned from this book, I have been able to walk away and now know that I will never find myself in such form of relationship ever again. – Nathalie Simmons

From the first line the author makes this book so easy to read and the personal documenting is utterly empowering. I couldn't put it away. To relate to so many of the authors words, and realise you are not alone, is life changing. From rollercoaster ride to teacup ride is the perfect analogy. – Alison Walker

How to contact Dr Mariette Jansen

Email: mariette@drdestress.co.uk

LinkedIn: www.linkedin.com/dr-mariette-jansen-dr-de-stress/

Website: www.drdestress.co.uk

Facebook: www.facebook.com/DrDeStresstips

Twitter: @Mariette_Jansen

Instagram: #narcissism_journey_book
#Mariette_Jansen

Prologue

This book is written from the perspective and perceptions of a victim. Feeling and being a victim is about feeling powerless and trapped. However, with knowledge and skills, a victim can turn into a victor.

This book is about and for victims of narcissistic abuse.

Narcissists can be described by their behaviours and attitudes. In this book, I have put together a checklist based on the five main attitudes of a narcissist.

Within the context of 'From Victim to Victor', a narcissist is someone who:

1. has a grandiose self-opinion,
2. has a sense of entitlement,
3. will attempt to control and manipulate,
4. cannot handle any form of criticism,
5. lacks empathy and emotional awareness.

If a person shows traits from each of these attitudes, we are talking about a narcissist.

This book

In this book I step away from clinical research, diagnosis and therapy models. I share my experiences and the experiences of others, defining narcissism from the point of view of the victims: the feelings and emotions towards a narcissist, the situations where the narcissistic approach is challenging, and practical ways to respond and deal with them in day-to-day life.

I have interviewed and connected with hundreds of people, who told me anecdotes and stories which helped me to build up the examples and narcissistic experiences presented in this book.

My experiences

My mother is a narcissist: a full-blown one – entitled, manipulative and cruel. It took me 40 years to come to the decision to cut her out of my life and it was a painful journey. I hope this book helps others to go through the process of recognition and decision-making a lot faster.

My mother had three children. I am the only one who is still alive, and I am the one with the voice. It feels as if I am speaking up for my brother and sister, as I frequently did when they were still around, and this book is a dedication to our bond. We had not only a sibling bond but also one of sharing similar harsh experiences yet never being able to freely talk about them. I am sharing on their behalf and with their support.

I was born in The Netherlands, went to university and worked in Utrecht. When I was 37, I moved to the UK to live with the love of my life. We started a family and now have two lovely boys and one female dog-daughter. The values in our family are love and respect and it comes with the freedom for every family member to be who they are. I am enjoying a lot of new positive experiences within our family unit and am very grateful for that. We enjoy being together and we have fun. I never had that. And it is absolutely wonderful.

Prologue

The nature of narcissism

Narcissism ranges from healthy and normal to pathological and malignant. It is related to the regulation of self-esteem and emotions. Narcissists are extremely insecure and aim to hide this insecurity and override it by attaining external validation. Narcissism can be the motivator to high achievements, but it easily co-occurs with pathological narcissistic traits and behaviour.

Usually, a narcissist doesn't suffer. They manipulate to get what they need and if that causes harm to others, they don't care. This is the result of their inability to step into someone else's shoes and imagine how they would feel. Their main focus is to get what they want. It is a rarity to see a narcissist in the therapy room, as they are convinced they are perfect and won't need to change. If life is not working, it is always down to others, who should change. Not them. That is one of the reasons that little is known about NPD (Narcissistic Personality Disorder).

From victim to victor

This book offers information, tips and hope. Hope for anyone who is a victim. You can get out. You can turn the tables and come out the other end. Victory is on the horizon. There is a price to pay, but there are huge rewards: freedom, being the authentic you and the knowledge that this will never ever happen to you again.

Thank you to all those brave people who shared their stories with me. It is not easy to start speaking about situations and other people, which have shame, guilt and anger attached to them. It is not easy to allow words to make your nightmare a reality. But I am grateful for all of you who found the courage.

Thank you to all those lovely friends (old and new) who supported the creation of this book through editing, reading, commenting, suggesting, asking, challenging, listening, questioning and genuinely connecting.

My greatest wish is that sharing my experiences and knowledge helps others to reduce their suffering, overcome the trauma more quickly and in the future avoid being intoxicated by the false allure of a narcissist.

Table of Contents

Introduction   9
Why this book?   9
What is a narcissist?   11
The five main characteristics of a narcissist   15

PART I:

Family Dynamics   19
Introduction   19
1. The fairy tale of the throne   19
2. The dominant-submissive household   23
3. Such a lovely family   25
4. Big brother   27
5. Little sis   31
6. Spineless father   33
7. Random childhood memories   35
8. Milestone memories   37
9. The lonely journey   40

Part II:

The Romantic Relationship   43
Introduction   43
1. Red flags indicating you are involved with a narcissist   45
2. The price you pay for the relationship   50
3. The Trauma Bond   52
4. Ending the relationship   53

Part III:

The Narcissist Checklist   59
Introduction   59
1. How to use the checklist   59
2. CATEGORY I: Grandiose view of self-importance   64
3. CATEGORY II: Has a sense of entitlement   92
4. CATEGORY III: Will control and manipulate   114
5. CATEGORY IV: Can't handle any form of criticism   148
6. CATEGORY V: Lacks empathy and emotional awareness   162

Part IV:

Frequently Asked Questions about Narcissism   185
Introduction   185

Part V:

Claim your victory   195
Introduction   195
1. Confusion   196
2. Stress and anxiety   197
3. The three key questions   199
4. Your toolbox   201

Part VI:

Summary   229

Epilogue   233
What's next?   233

About the Author   235

Bibliography and references   238

Introduction

Why this book?

My father died and I instantly had a sense of freedom. I felt free to breathe just for me, free to only watch out for myself and my family, free to write about the biggest challenge in my life: my mother.

Even though I had chosen to not have her in my life, there was sometimes contact as I still felt a sense of responsibility to look out for my dad. But with him gone, that responsibility went, leaving me truly cut off from her.

Why am I writing about my mother, you might ask?

My mother has NPD and through this, she made her whole family suffer. Narcissists are cruel, manipulative and clever. They are also very skilful at controlling others in such a subtle manner that it is difficult to clearly point it out. Moving away from a narcissist is almost impossible without support. They won't want to let you go.

My journey was painful and enriching, frustrating and liberating, and always involved a lot of emotional effort.

I wrote this book with two aims:

1. The first aim is to support people who are living with a narcissist or have a narcissist in their life and want to understand more of what is happening in their situation and to them.

2. The second aim is to educate people who have no direct experiences with a narcissist but are interested in learning more.

It was a bonus that writing about the subject and my experiences was quite cathartic and I felt much lighter as a result.

This book is divided into six parts:

- **Part I** is 'all about me' and my experiences in the dysfunctional family I grew up in. I hope it gives a feel for how my family operated. It is not my life story but a series of impressions and situations.
- **Part II** is about narcissistic romantic relationships.
- **Part III** will take you through the checklist of narcissistic traits. This will help you to recognise narcissistic behaviour and how you are affected.
- **Part IV** Frequently Asked Questions and answers.
- **Part V** Tips, tools and techniques.
- **Part VI** Summary.

I have tried to keep it light and accessible and most of the content is based on my experience.

All through the book, you will find tips on how to deal with people and situations in order to keep yourself safe and sane. These tips are not only helpful when facing a narcissist, but also when you are dealing with narcissistic behaviour.

How to use this book?

It is up to you to choose how to make the most of this book. It will depend on what you want to get out of it.

If you want to understand clearly what narcissism is and how this condition manifests in people, read the book and find your answers.

Introduction

If you want to check out if people in your life are narcissists and how they affect you, you will benefit from working through the checklist. You can use the space allocated in this book, buy a separate notebook or order the workbook, designed to guide you through the exercises.

If you want to learn how to respond and deal with narcissists in your life in a way that keeps yourself and your loved ones safe, read about the different tools and techniques and start applying them. One at the time. And you can return to the book time and again. Make notes about situations and your narcissist, so you have an ongoing record of what worked and what didn't.

In 2000, I became a psychotherapist and in 2011 a life coach. It was a way of using my personal growth and development in a profession where I could help others going through challenging processes. In my private practice, I have had more and more clients who are living with a narcissist and it is painful to recognise my old struggle in their current one. However, it is also wonderful to be able to support them from a full understanding. I am convinced that has helped many to recover quicker.

I wish that this book is a support, a motivator and provides guidance for anyone who needs it. I know there are many of us around.

What is a narcissist?

Many labels are used and misused for the sake of clarity. However, they are often confusing as the character and content of each label knows endless variations.

When it comes to narcissism, from time to time every single one of us will show some of the 50 narcissistic traits, as defined in my checklist. Just showing one single trait doesn't qualify someone as a narcissist. However, as these traits are aiming to control others, it is helpful to recognise them and find a response that will keep yourself protected from the resulting manipulation.

Not a lot is known about the specific source of NPD. But it seems that there is a link with childhood experiences and what are called unhealthy attachments.

Emotionally healthy children have grown up with a sense of security. They felt loved, safe through the loving attitude and actions of parents and carers. They were able to build a sense of self and confidence, which made them ready to venture out into the world.

When a child lacks that security, a distorted picture of their self is created. They might believe they are not worthy of love and not capable of attracting it. To deny this unpleasant state, their actions focus on proving themselves wrong. They create situations which will confirm that they are lovable and worthy. However, deep down inside, they don't believe it, regardless of how much confirmation they receive.

Most narcissists have grown up with this insecurity and confusion. There might have been a cold parent who pushed them away and another one who would spoil them rotten. They might not have been seen and/or heard. They might have been ignored and/or neglected.

Another idea is that there is a genetic element to the disorder. If parents or grandparents are NPD, the condition might have been inherited.

Dr Ramani, an American psychologist who specialises in narcissism, claims that 10 to 15% of the population is narcissistic, of which 80% are male.

Her claim is not based on scientific research as the measurement tools for narcissism are not scientific and factual.

One of the things that sets a narcissist apart from 'normal' people is that they don't experience emotions, other than anger, fear, envy and hate. These negative emotions help them to feel detached from others and safe.

What causes narcissism?

There is limited research on the causes of narcissism. But there are indications that the following elements might have an impact on how people 'develop' their narcissism:

1. Brain wiring

A group of German researchers have proven that we can see narcissism in the brain. Brain scans of people with Narcissistic Personality Disorder (NPD) showed that they have less brain matter in areas associated with emotional empathy (bilateral anterior insula, anterior and median parts of the cingulate cortex, and the supplementary motor area). There might be a genetic element to this.

2. Insecure attachments

Children who grow up with parents or carers who don't give them emotional security will often develop an insecure attachment. Cold, dismissive and critical parents will encourage insecure attachments. This will lead in later life to dysfunctional emotional relationships, low confidence and a low sense of self.

3. Upbringing and modelling

We don't know what we have never seen. Growing up in a dysfunctional family makes dysfunction the norm and copying the known behaviour is very common.

4. Positive parenting

Bringing up children with positive guidance, nurturing and protection, aims to create balanced adults. However, children who are protected from criticism and challenges might develop grandiose ideas about themselves as, they have always received the feedback that 'the sun shines out of their bottom'.

Safe through their mask

The narcissistic self is very fragile. It has never been developed, but from an early age onwards, it has been masked by certain types of behaviour. Their biggest fear is to be seen for who they are (unlovable), and they will do anything to prevent that from happening. They are continually on the look-out for danger and when they spot it, their fear kicks in. A natural response to fear is anger. Imagine you are in a car and another car nearly hits you. Your initial feeling is fear, next you will get angry with the other driver who put you in danger.

When a narcissist perceives danger and they react aggressively through disagreeing, contradicting or challenging others around them. They feel the threat might reveal their fragile ego, and use anger as a way of protection. Following, they hate people who put them in that scary position and set out to control and punish them.

Feeding their ego

As their ego is tiny, they strive to make it bigger and more important through Narcissistic Supply: receiving attention and admiration. One narcissist said during an interview that this was his biggest addiction: the need for confirmation. It was more important than money or anything else. And he would do anything to get it. Narcissistic Supply is their life force, their addiction, to be provided by other people.

The five main characteristics of a narcissist

1. **A grandiose view of themselves.** They are convinced that they are fabulous, interesting, top-dog and the centre of not just their universe but also everybody else's. They make this clear whenever they feel necessary. Centre stage is where they belong.

2. **A sense of entitlement.** They consider themselves to be so interesting and special, they believe they are entitled to special treatment. They feel there is no need for them to appreciate what others do or to say thank you. Others are there to serve them.

3. **They control and manipulate.** They apply a range of clever and effective techniques seeking attention, admiration and confirmation.

4. **They can't handle criticism.** Any form of negative feedback infuriates a narcissist and sparks nasty behaviour. This makes it impossible to discuss situations and events in an honest and open manner. They are convinced it is always the fault of others and never theirs. It is also the reason that there is limited scientific research on NPD,

as a narcissist is convinced that if someone is wrong, it is never them.

5. **Lack of empathy and emotional awareness.** They have no idea what other people might feel, what they struggle with or what they need support with. Narcissists are cold and able to be incredibly cruel.

If someone shows all five of the above characteristics, they are most likely suffering from NPD. They will cause harm and pain to others in order to get their Narcissistic Supply. Some powerful people are thought to be narcissists, such as Steve Jobs, Donald Trump and Madonna.

Narcissistic behaviour can vary from being selfish and self-obsessed to being cocky, arrogant or manipulative.

Being driven and focussed might spark narcissistic behaviour, without making the person with that behaviour a narcissist.

Think of an athlete who trains to get to the Olympics. They focus their physical, mental and emotional energy on their athletic performance. There is no time or energy to spend on others. Does that make them a narcissist or just a driven athlete?

Think of a businessman, who runs a multi-national corporation. His job is all about processes and systems and he spends most of his time trying to solve serious problems. When he comes home, he doesn't want to spend time on other people's problems. Not even his wife's ones. He just wants to switch off and relax. Does that make him a narcissist or just a bad husband?

I have created a checklist of 50 personality traits and discussed these with hundreds of people who have experienced the influence of a narcissist in their lives. Every single narcissist ticked at least 40 of those traits, which is a strong indication you are dealing with one.

People who do not have NPD can still be unpleasant or toxic and tick a few checkpoints on the list. Being able to recognise controlling or manipulating behaviour is always helpful if you want to be in control of yourself and your situation.

How do you know you are dealing with a narcissist?

When you are in contact with a narcissist, you might feel uneasy around them. Something isn't quite right. But in the first instance, you won't be able to put your finger on it. They might confuse you, being unkind or unpleasant in a subtle way. You might think about them trying to figure it out. They might be upset because you don't agree with them.

These are all pointers.

PART I:
Family Dynamics

Introduction

In this chapter I present you with the fairy tale of my family, followed by a short introduction of the type of dysfunctional family that is created by narcissistic parents. This is followed by my perception of events within the family. First of all, the perfect family – how my brother, sister and father fitted in and a range of little stories.

1. The fairy tale of the throne

Once upon a time, there was a girl who thought she was the one who deserved the best. Always. She also decided to make it her life purpose to get the best, even if it was at the expense of others.

The little girl grew up and developed the skill of obtaining the best as she was convinced she was the best: the prettiest in her family, clever at school and the teacher's pet. She turned into a very powerful person who was very skilful at disguising her real nature. She presented herself as beautiful, loving, caring and fun. In reality, she was nasty, selfish, cold and manipulative.

She was like a powerful, iron-fisted queen.

A queen should sit on a throne, and she designed a beautiful throne for herself. It was gold and shiny and placed on a stepped square platform. From her high position, she could control anyone and everything that went on beneath her.

Then she met her prince. He couldn't become a king, as this would meand he'd sit at her level and he might overshadow her, which would be unacceptable. The prince she chose was a soft-hearted, kind man. He was quite insecure, didn't have a lot of experience with women and thought the queen was the bee's knees. Just what she loved.

The prince adored her and couldn't see or find fault.

Life was good for the queen and prince, as they both got what they needed. She felt admired and put on a pedestal (where she was convinced, she belonged) and he couldn't believe that someone like her had fallen in love with someone like him. The couple soon became a family when baby number one arrived. A little prince. Two little princesses followed, and the family was then complete.

The queen was comfortable, she felt in control and knew her position was grand. Her throne was in a steady position and her prince and babies formed a team of four who continuously polished her beautiful throne. As each of them was responsible for one side of the square platform, they were not able to really see each other and communicate. Everything was overseen and controlled by the queen. If someone didn't perform up to her standards, she let them know. Her sharp voice, harsh words and punishments were painful and all four of the polishers tried to avoid upsetting her.

Sometimes they felt like rebelling, but as they couldn't reach the other members of the team, it felt too dangerous to do it by themselves. The queen had no idea what was going on in the heads and hearts of the team members and she really didn't care. As long as she was positioned on a shiny throne, she was happy.

The husband prince loved polishing and admired the queen so much that he started to copy her behaviour. He became her biggest ally on the lower level and supported her requirements towards the children. When she overlooked something, he would address it.

It was as if all of them were cursed by the queen. They were under her spell and there was no way out. The best survival mechanism seemed to be to accommodate her.

They didn't even allow the thought of running away and leaving. They just kept their heads down.

After a few years, the older princess started to protest. It didn't feel good to surrender to fate and she started to stand up to the queen. To no avail. When she spoke up, she was not listened to but put down. 'What a ridiculous remark and how dare you speak like that.' Punishment would follow: the silent dismissive treatment from the queen and the sad disappointment of the big prince. The princess felt awful and her confidence crumbled.

She didn't give up. She tried to discuss her feelings, she wanted so desperately to connect with both the prince and the queen. But whatever she tried, it seemed that she couldn't reach either; they didn't understand and told her she was hysterical and mad.

After a few years of trying, the princess closed down inside. She stopped thinking as there was no point, and she stopped feeling as it was too painful. The void that this created was being filled with food. She developed a serious eating disorder that kept her mind away from the painful experiences under the throne.

When she got older, the princess left the throne and moved somewhere else. But emotionally, she was still very much connected to it and continued to hope to connect to the queen. When she wasn't successful, she started to talk to professionals, had therapy, read books and put in endless effort to create a connection.

Finally, after 40 years of trying, at the age of 58, she called it a day. She surrendered and gave up hope. There would never be a loving and healthy relationship with the queen. The princess stepped away from the throne. Never to return. It was a painful process but at last, she was free. She had the mental space to become herself and surround herself with positive people and experiences. At last, she could live an authentic life and be of service to others, instead of servicing the queen.

The courageous princess didn't keep her experiences to herself and started to share them with other people. She discovered that there were so many other queens and kings who demanded polishing from their family and friends. She had discovered how to break the spell, and she now helped others to break free in less time than it took her. The princess lived a fulfilling life, happy ever after.

The queen stayed on her throne. She became the only 'occupant' as the little prince, the youngest princess and her husband prince had all passed away within a few years of each other. With no one around to do the polishing, the throne became dull, unimpressive and started to crumble.

Metaphor

The queen is my mother. A woman cursed with a cold heart and a narcissistic personality. Only a few years ago, I discovered more about narcissism. It helped me to understand what was going on, to manage my hopes and expectations, and I was able to fully process the intense hurt and pain that she caused me.

Narcissists are toxic. They have the skill to make other people feel inferior – being in the lower position of the throne. They are clever and make others work for them – the constant polishing. They are manipulative and embrace the 'divide and rule' philosophy – hence the separate position of all polishers. There is no chance of ganging up or direct communication.

This story has a happy ending and everything I experienced and learned on the way is shared in this book. I hope you can recognise your queen or king and are able to break free.

Sooner rather than later.

2. The dominant-submissive household

Families make and break people. The family or lack of family is the first point of reference for a baby and infant. It informs them of hierarchies, roles, values and patterns of interactions and behaviour. The child creates a sense of self within the context of the family's dynamics. If a family is not a safe environment, a sense of self will be formed by the primary need to survive instead of by the healthy development of individual traits. Children are limited in their experiences. They are familiar with their family and embrace what happens in that context as normality. If that normality is toxic, their development will be strongly influenced and it might lead to mental and emotional issues later in life.

There are several dysfunctional family dynamics and when one or both parents are narcissists, the household becomes a dominant-submissive one where one parent dictates and the other one is passively obedient. The dictator doesn't consider the wishes of other family members and there is a lot of underlying tension and anger. The family dynamics revolve around the needs, wants, desires and dramas of the parent. Children are viewed as things that need to be controlled, used and manipulated. Everyone suffers in silence.

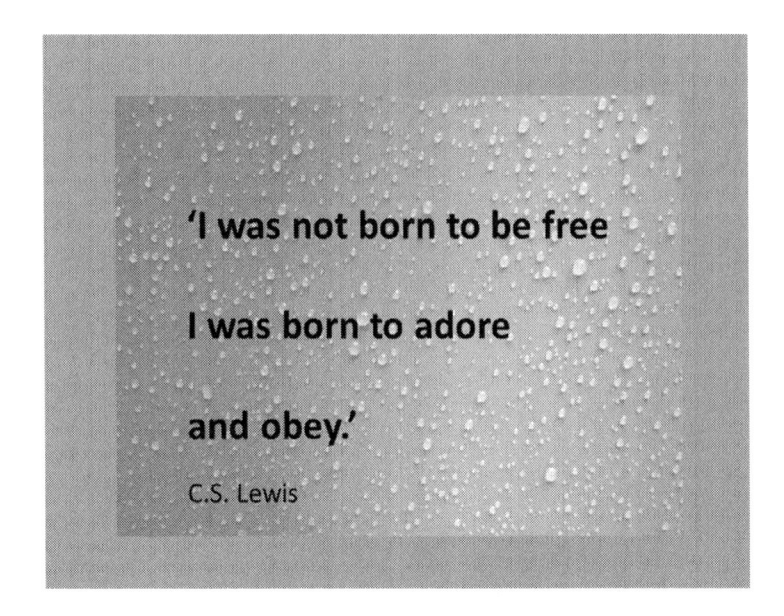

> 'I was not born to be free
>
> I was born to adore
>
> and obey.'
>
> C.S. Lewis

Signs of a dominant-submissive family:

- Emotional neglect
- Parents are controlling and domineering
- Infantilisation
- Not allowing the child to grow up, so they are easier to manipulate.
- No discipline but punishment. Discipline is pro-active and a tool for teaching, whereas punishment is a tool to control.
- Judgment and criticism

Children have no way of knowing that they are in a toxic family. But they can feel something isn't right. That certainly was the case for me and for a lot of people I have spoken to.

Family Dynamics

By sharing the story about my family, I hope to give an insight and understanding of how a narcissist influences their family members. How they deal with challenges, or not. How they manipulate and twist. How they keep the control going. It is personal and it might not be of interest to you, but if you want to have a peep into a dysfunctional family, go ahead.

3. Such a lovely family

The narcissistic parent is perfect and of course, so is their family. My parents spent a lot of time and effort presenting our perfect family to the outside world. The focus was to show us off as a lovely family. They created lots of different scenarios that served this purpose. They knew best, and they would make the decisions. Democracy wasn't applied in 'such a lovely family'.

A few examples

My father started a children's choir at the church. He was a reasonable pianist and all three of us children played the piano and had to select a second instrument. Mine was the traverso, the flute, and I played with the choir and even did solos at the start and end of the service. My brother played the drums to accompany the choir. My younger sister (half-heartedly) played the guitar and reluctantly joined the team. From the outside, it looked wonderful.

Such a lovely family

Everyone had to play tennis. With each other. We had these family tennis sessions. I am not sure if I know any other families who were so 'close' on the tennis court. I remember coming home from university at the weekend and having to play tennis from 4 till 6 on Saturday with my parents and my brother. There was no choice. Seeing your friends at that time?

How could you deny your parents, who are doing everything for you, the pleasure of playing tennis?

Such a lovely family

We, as children, were 'offered' a family skiing holiday when my brother was 25, I was 24 and my sister was 21. The offer consisted of the ski pass, accommodation and food. What we were expected to pay for was our travel, ski lessons (which we couldn't afford but desperately needed) and meals out as an appropriate 'thank you'.

Another way of 'paying' for the holiday was to keep our parents company and ski together, eat together and go to bed at the same time as them. It was a holiday that was totally controlled by them. On reflection, it would have been cheaper and much more fun to go skiing without them.

Such a lovely family

I was told that my mother was my best friend when I was a teenager. I didn't have a lot of teenage friends. The relationship with my BFF (Best Friend Forever) from primary school was killed off by my mother. When my BFF got friendly with another girl, I was upset by the girl's politics. My mother was there, telling me that friendships were useless, they never lasted. I should not engage with BFF. It wouldn't work. It was family that counted. The rest of the world was not to be trusted. Clearly she would know because she didn't have any girlfriends. Nor had my dad any male friends. With my lack of friends, my mother stepped up to claim me as her best friend and I went with it.

Such a lovely family

It was very important that we were that lovely family, where everything was loving and harmonious. To the outside world. But we definitely weren't experiencing love, fun and harmony on the inside. The real world, the real family, was very different. Lots of arguments, protests, rebellion, but it always ended up with my parents getting their way.

However, if you have not known anything different and were told time and again how wonderful your family was, why wouldn't you believe that you were lucky to be part of such 'a lovely family'?

> My mother, the super narcissist, has taken a lot away from me, but she has given me a precious present: resilience, insights and a positive mindset.
>
> Dr Mariette Jansen

4. Big brother

Big brother wrecked it for his mother.

Big time.

My mother was one of three sisters and she married the best-looking man, with the best status profession. He bought her the biggest house of the three and she was the first to have a baby. Ahead of the game in competing with the sisterhood.

But my brother Janjo destroyed that picture because he had physical and learning disabilities.

Unfortunately, it was due to my parents' attitude that this happened. They had opted for a home birth for their first child. However, my mother passed her due date and they were strongly advised to give birth at the hospital. Overdue babies are big, much harder work to deliver and the chances of complications are significantly higher. My parents were adamant their baby was going to be born at home. The birth wasn't easy and after hours of labour, it became clear that extra support was needed. An ambulance was called. Sadly, by then, tragedy had already struck. My brother was stuck in the birth canal. He couldn't get out and suffered from lack of oxygen with brain damage as a result. This manifested itself in learning difficulties. He was on the autistic spectrum and his physical coordination was quite unbalanced. From a very young age, people looked at him and asked themselves, 'What is the matter with this boy? Is he all right?' As in 'normal'?

I don't think my mother ever forgave my brother for shattering her dream world. I can't remember seeing any photos of just her and him together.

Just 14 months after Janjo's birth, I popped into the world. Interestingly, this time a home birth was not considered and my mother was induced two weeks before her due date. Why was that?

Me and my big brother were a team. I was quite a feisty little number and with only a small age difference, we did things together. Intuitively I looked after him from a very young age. I felt he needed me, I needed to protect him and make sure he was safe. Nobody told me anything about his condition until I was 12, and the information came with a huge reprimand.

Family Dynamics

One of those things we did together, was to attend a music camp during the summer. We learned how to make a bamboo flute, did sports, played music and games and had a good time. At a reunion of one of those holiday camps, I remember clearly that I didn't want to focus on my brother the whole day. It was a conscious decision. Maybe these were the thoughts of a rebellious teenager? I made sure I shared our sweets, he got his drinks, but for the rest of the time, I was off partying. This behaviour was reported back to my parents a few days later and I was summoned into my mother's 'music room'. To be told off, to be called selfish, disgusting and made to feel like a horrible person. It was then that I asked why he needed looking after – something I had been doing all of my life anyway. I got her 'story'. How the medical staff had made a mistake with the forceps and had damaged his brain. I didn't know it wasn't the truth, but at least I had an explanation.

He started working at the age of 16 in a 'social factory'. Work was the place where he could be himself, surrounded by other people who all had their own particular disability and were accepted and respected as they were. I am convinced that that was one of the reasons he adored his work.

When he was 50, my parents were fed up with him living with them and being around all the time. They found him a house not far from theirs and told him to buy it. He moved out to live independently but it became clear quickly that he wasn't able to live by himself. People who cared for him, my sister and I, were really concerned. Discussing any options with my parents was useless. 'You don't know anything about this. We know best.'

The situation continued for ten years before it all went wrong for my parents, thanks to two people who were asked to take over Janjo's care. Cousin Tim looked after my brother's finances, cousin Hans looked after his social and emotional well-being.

Hans brought to light that my brother was in a bad place. Janjo felt lonely, didn't feel welcome at the parental home, felt pushed into errands he didn't want to do… And the reason he didn't want to do them was that he actually wasn't physically able to do them. He was overweight, possibly diabetic but also had developed a heart condition. Which was alluded to by my parents as 'He is so lazy; he doesn't want to walk more than 100 meters and then he sits down'. When I spoke to them about it, I told them to be kind, that no one would make up being that tired. Yet again, would they listen?

Hans managed to get him into sheltered housing and for the first time ever, he felt at home where he lived. He lived with people who were severely disabled, some in complicated wheelchairs, some not able to eat by themselves or even speak and he was part of their group. He belonged there and it was a clear indication of his disability. For him, at last, like at work, he was in an environment where he could be himself, relaxed and happy. At last. Being good enough.

For my mother, it was a defeat.

Hans and Tim got a good insight into what was going on between my parents and my brother and soon they decided to stop their involvement. The reason was that my parents were taking money from Janjo. Unethical and illegal. My father had gambled on the stock market and lost most of his money. On top of that, they used Janjo's account to pay for their utilities and outrageous financial gifts (like £1000 for Mother's Day). They tried to sell his house cheaply to a 'supporter' (someone on benefits with lots of time, who helped my parents out with lifts, gardening, shopping, being a handyman in return for cash), which would have left my brother with a huge debt.

These actions were undertaken by people who had told me all my life: 'You can't trust anyone. People are always taking money from others, and especially vulnerable people like your brother.'

I wasn't able to be in contact with my brother as my parents had told him what a nasty person I was and if he was in touch, they would turn their back on him. He didn't have any choice but to give them their way.

My parents, at the age of 86, got a court order for financial and emotional abuse, which ended their parental responsibility. It was about time.

I had tried to cut the cord with them several times but had always given in after a while. Feeling sorry for them, wanting to look after my siblings, trying to be kind, but when this hypocritical and unethical behaviour came to light, it was easy for me to close the door forever. I was done. They overstepped the mark so clearly that there was no going back.

5. Little sis

My sister Anneke was three and a half years younger than me. We never developed a very close relationship. 'Two different flowers, growing in the same border'. It was partly due to our differences and partly due to my mother's attempts to keep us apart.

She was a rebel, didn't care, was stalwart and independent. I was compliant, the good girl, looking for love and confirmation. She shrugged her shoulders; I did my best to comply. I can imagine how irritating that must have been for her. During the first 14 years of her life, I was the golden child. I got more attention than she did. I also felt more rejection but how could she know that?

Anneke became a tennis coach. That didn't give her bonus points from my mother. Her tennis friends became her family. The place where she was appreciated and loved for who she was.

Being gay was another big disappointment. Instead of accepting the fact, my mother denied it. 'She just hasn't met the right man. She always said that she wanted a man like her father, so I know she is not into women.' Did she ever say she wanted a husband like my father? Or did my mother need to 'hear' that to confirm that she, again, had the best possible option? The word lesbian never passed her lips, ever. In her view of the world, it simply wasn't true, and she had yet another secret to hide.

When Anneke introduced her girlfriend, my mother hated her with a vengeance. I don't think Marijke took any nonsense from her and was very assertive. It would have caused my sister a lot of aggravation. Who to choose? Who to support? The relationship didn't last and there never was another girl openly on the scene. How much of this was down to my mother?

Anneke developed a progressive lung disease and needed oxygen. A few years later she was 'lucky' to have a double lung transplant and worked hard on her recovery. She had her network of tennis friends, her surrogate family, and me, who helped her through the tough times. My parents were nowhere to be seen.

Life was not meant to be for my sister. After a cancer scare in November 2014, she went through painful treatment, got the all-clear in February, only to discover that she had developed lung cancer. Three weeks later she was gone. Aged 52.

Sad. Sad. Sad.

Who said that life was fair? In Apeldoorn, where Anneke lived all her life and gave a lot of energy to tennis, she is living on in the AJT ('Anneke Jansen Tennis') – a tennis school at the club where she felt at home.

A legacy to be proud of.
A little sis to be proud of.

6. Spineless father

My father lost himself through and in the relationship with his wife, my mother. He never stood up for himself, he looked up to her to get confirmation that he had done the right things and only resisted her when he tried to protect my sister.

A few years ago, I had a tarot card reading. The reader picked up family cards and she described my mother. I nodded as it was spot on. Then she picked a card for my father and said surprised: 'This is exactly the same as your mother'. That is precisely what had happened. My father had been absorbed and assimilated by my mother.

My father had a very sheltered upbringing and was green as grass when he met my mother at the age of 25.

When a narcissist has decided on their partner, it becomes a whirlwind courting time. No time to lose to secure the treasure. This is what happened with my parents. They got married within a year of meeting each other.

How romantic.

My grandmother apparently found it hard to smile during the wedding day. She probably had the measure of my mother and was concerned about my father's happiness. I actually wonder if he was unhappy? I don't think he had any idea of the type of person my mother was and he adored her and felt happy as long as he got her attention and approval. Like a dog who is happy to be with their owner, even though they are treated badly. My father started to copy my mother's behaviour and turned himself into a narcissist.

They presented themselves as the perfect couple.

Of course.

One of the things I had never realised was how they made a real statement with birthday presents for my mother. Always given in the presence of friends and family. My father would sit behind the piano. She would stand close by and he would serenade her with a song he had especially written for her before handing over the present. In my own family now, we give each other presents in private. It is nobody else's business. For my parents, gift-giving was a big part of showing off.

No one really knew my father.

Apart from that he was weak, served my mother, ignored his children, loved his work and died at the age of 88.

> **I have a dream.**
> A dream that will stay a dream forever.
> It is about me and my dad.
> Just him and me, doing something together.
> It couldn't happen.
> He couldn't prefer me over her, my mother.
> Not when I was a little girl,
> Not when I was a grown-up.
> We never had a real relationship.
> Another 'take-away' from my narcissistic mother.
>
> Dr Mariette Jansen

7. Random childhood memories

Did I have a great childhood? I was told time and again that our family was the best. Why wouldn't I believe it? I didn't know any other families, and my mother kept telling me how strange other people were, how bad, how you couldn't trust them… And I guess that kept me thinking how lucky I was to be in our setting. I knew there wasn't a lot of laughter and lightness in our house. Life is a serious matter and there were lots of rules and conditions to live by and not a lot of support and warmth.

Whenever I am asked to picture myself as a child (this is what happens in therapy a lot and as I have had a lot, I know this picture very well), it's there straight away. It is a picture of a little girl in a pretty pink dress, sitting on a dark wooden floor on her nappy bottom. There is space around her from every side and she feels very unsafe. No shelter, nowhere to hide. The little girl is sitting straight and just feels the loneliness. There is no one there for her, nothing to turn to, she literally just has to sit it out in the cold in that big space.

The first day I went to primary school – aged six – I went on my little red bike, all by myself. I met the other kids who had arrived with their mums and some even with both parents. After all, this is a big day in the life of a parent and a child. For me, it was a change I just had to get on with.

I must have known subconsciously that I didn't belong in my family.

When my parents went skiing together, they left me with friends: a couple who had a daughter who was a few years older than I was. That was fantastic. Being around a girl who was allowed make-up and talked about music and maybe even boys was a dream for any young teenager. I loved Leah and I loved Aunt (Tante) Hennie, her mum, even more. She smiled a lot, was very caring, fed her little dog treats and sent me to school with a treat as well – a snack for break time. I had never ever been given a snack to take to school. She wrapped some cookies or flapjacks in aluminium foil, and to this day, using aluminium foil warms my heart. The last evening of the two weeks I spent with that family we were all in front of the television nibbling on crisps, which was also a big treat in those days. My heart felt heavy. Heavy and sad. This lovely time was coming to an end. I didn't want it to end. I followed Tante Hennie into the kitchen and burst into tears. 'I don't want to go home. I want to stay here. I am so happy here. Why do I have to leave?' My heart was broken. Tante Hennie held me close to her. I don't know what was going on in her mind, but I was desperate. Of course, the next day I had to jump on my bike with a bag of clothes to go home with a heart full of sadness.

I loved reading. Anything. But my favourite at one time was the Belinda-series. For a start, the name Belinda was so exotic and mysterious and her family was very different from mine. When she passed her high school exams, her dad took her out shopping to buy her a special dress. After the shopping spree they went out to a restaurant. I read that with pain in my heart. I wished my father would do that with me. Just me. But that would never happen. My mother would always be there. She would not allow the two of us to go out and maybe discuss her…

My father was very keen on his music and the moments I really felt connected with him were when we played together. Me on my flute, he on the piano. Interestingly, we could never play for too long, as my mother would interrupt and tell us to get on with the next part of the day. Coffee together or a meal or anything that would break up the union my father and I had built up.

At school I was a good student. I worked hard and had reasonably good results. I was particularly proud when I came home with the result for a history test – a 9, the equivalent of an A*. Very happily I shared my results at the table during our evening meal. The feedback I got was dismissive, 'It is nothing to be proud of because if you have the brain, the least you can do is to use it. It is your obligation. Not everybody has brains…' It left me deflated but I also had a sense that something wasn't right. Did I not work really hard to get it? Could I not get praise for that? It felt like a no-win situation: did I not have good results? I was lazy but if I had good results, it was wrong to be pleased with them. The fact that I still remember this means it was really big for me.

I didn't realise it at the time, but I was continuously anxious. Now I understand that there was hardly a safe place in my life. Even with friends from school, my mother would point out time and again that I was mad to trust them. Any little quarrel was an invitation for her to tell me that the only people you can trust are your close family.

A huge part of my anxiety had to do with my mother's continual dismissive responses to me. The things I longed for most in my life were her approval and her love, her being kind to me; but for some reason, I was never good enough, not loveable.

8. Milestone memories

My mother will tell you that I completely changed after I left home to go to university. She felt I had been brainwashed. The lovely accommodating girl had disappeared and turned into a monster.

What really happened was that I became more aware of the things that happened in my family that weren't right. I felt responsible for everybody's happiness and fought to correct things or at least make them better.

Important moments mark the process

A few weeks into my new life as a student, I shared with my parents a situation of one of my new friends. I was shocked by the coldness of their reaction. My friend was terribly upset because her boyfriend had betrayed her. He was married but had told her, hand on heart, that he was in a divorce situation, which unfortunately didn't materialise as he was going to have a baby with his wife. When my friend heard this news, she was utterly devastated. And so was I, for her. So much pain and sadness. I felt upset on her behalf. My parents, however, called her a slut (having an affair with a married man), him a bastard and said it was her own fault. End of story. This was the first time I was aware of their total lack of empathy.

I was controlled through money. They gave me a minimal amount each week, even though they easily could afford more. I was expected to come home each weekend. They paid my travel money and my weekly allowance. If I didn't go home, I didn't get any money. Without discussing it with me, my parents bought a place in my student town, where I could live with two other students. They made me responsible for collecting the rent and when it wasn't paid, they requested me to pay it. I also had to pay for small repairs and the installation of a telephone, so I could call them.

By then, I had found a part-time PR job and, thanks to my own ingenuity and performance, managed to get a pay rise. When I happily shared this positive development with my parents, they told me they would now charge me rent. Within a month, I found alternative accommodation and left it to them to sort their place out (not mine anymore).

Family Dynamics

There were regular occurrences which made me feel my parents acted against me, instead of being supportive.

I wrote a letter, which shared in detail how I felt, what didn't feel right to me and what I would like to change. I made sure it arrived before the weekend. I then went home churned with nerves. My father picked me up from the station – as always about 5-10 minutes late – and when we were home, I asked my parents if they received my letter. 'Oh, that one… Yes. But it is just a hysterical and untrue recall of situations. We have nothing to say.' The desperation hit me. Again.

Over the years, I tried different approaches. To no avail. And also, I regularly tried to stop any contact. However, the sense of responsibility for my brother and sister drove me back time and again.

My parents kept on saying to me: 'We don't understand what we did wrong. Why don't you be clear about it?' There are only so many ways you can explain the same situation to people who don't listen… I know now that they would never understand because they didn't want to. When it became clear that my parents had stolen money from my brother, I was so disgusted that I wasn't prepared to let them into my life anymore. And I closed the final curtain.

Finally, after 40 years of fighting I came to the conclusion of exclusion: the decision and subsequent action were that I didn't want to be in touch with either of my parents ever again. I took the decision and closed the final curtain.

The sense of freedom it gives me is incredible. Not having their toxic presence in my life means it is filled with joy, creativity and fun, instead of guilt, sadness and frustration.

9. The lonely journey

Breaking away from my narcissistic situation has been a lonely journey. I felt very alone from a young age but didn't know what that was about. I thought it was just me being strange and different. Later on, incident after incident made me aware that something wasn't right about my family.

It was difficult to find people to talk to. Everyone always seemed to defend my parents. Especially if I spoke about my mother, I would often get an answer along the lines of 'she doesn't mean it' or 'she must have had a terrible upbringing' and 'I am sure she loves you'. There was seldom an acknowledgement of her strange and unkind behaviour.

It seemed important to others to say that I should make peace. Telling me I should be the bigger person and 'get over it'. 'You only have one mother and you have to try to make it work' and 'all parents make mistakes. Wait till you are a parent.'

Well, I became a parent. Much to my own surprise, the maternal urge hit me when I was 39. Just in time. And I have made mistakes, but I have not committed the fundamental error of manipulating my children – lying, rejecting, neglecting, using and abusing, putting them down and confusing them.

Most people refused to believe what I was telling them. The person who caused all the pain kept on telling me she hadn't done anything wrong; so, the only solution seemed to be to get over it.

The abusive nature of the relationship with my parents is difficult to understand because, from a normal perspective, it is impossible to understand a narcissist. And what we don't understand is easily dismissed. I felt horrible whenever I was in contact with my mother. The best times were when I had decided to not be in touch and I learned it was best to not talk about her or my situation with others.

I knew a reconciliation wasn't the answer, but for most people that would be the best thing. Not when you are dealing with a narcissist though.

Part II:
The Romantic Relationship

Introduction

In the first chapter, I aimed to give an impression of life with a narcissistic parent. The child will think that their parents and family are normal, as they haven't experienced anything different yet. The child will also think they have no value unless they adhere to the demands of their narcissistic parent. Without unconditional love, they will have doubts, lack confidence and look for confirmation from an external source. However, this is their sense of normality. It is only later in life, when the child has escaped the family home with all its pressures, that he or she might start to discover different types of relationships, finally having the space to develop themselves.

It is not unusual for a child with narcissistic parents to find themselves in a romantic relationship with a narcissist. It is the familiarity of the relationship that attracts.

People look for partners that complement them. The relationship fills a need or a lack. The dreamer will feel attracted to the down-to-earth partner, the chaotic person falls in the love with the well-organised one, etc.

Research shows that highly empathic people and narcissists are often drawn to each other and show polar opposites in their brain activity, which might explain the attraction. Empathic people have a lot of compassion and understanding to give, are usually quite compliant and tend to 'rescue' others. Narcissists thrive on someone worshipping them and are keen to control another person. They will get that from an empathic partner. The kind and empathic partner will allow the narcissist to play out all their traits and then forgive them, hoping things will change. While they lose themselves in the process.

People who grew up with a narcissistic parent are susceptible to falling for a narcissist. They are familiar with the pattern of abuse and won't see it as unhealthy. In a lot of cases, like mine, the child has been trying to build a loving relationship with the narcissistic parent. To no avail. In order to look for healing, they will look for a similar situation, where they get the chance to create with their partner precisely what they wanted to create with their parent. Needless to say, this doesn't work. I was in a steady nine-year relationship with my new 'mother', represented by my partner. And I'm glad I got out of it.

To fall in love and find yourself in a romantic relationship with a narcissist is a life-changing experience. Often people change into someone they don't recognise.

'I used to be so confident. What has happened to me?'

'I used to be so relaxed. Now I spend so much time thinking about my partner and our relationship. It seems to consume all my mental energy.'

'I am so lucky to have him or her as I am such a difficult person to live with.'

The narcissist follows a pattern to cement the relationship and get their partner 'hooked'. Then the confusion and control start. Confusion is a great foundation for successful control. It undermines confidence and an insecure person is a great target. Once you are in the relationship, it is very, very, very difficult to get out.

1. Red flags indicating you are involved with a narcissist

When you fall in love, life couldn't be better. You feel beautiful both on the inside and outside and are on top of the world. It's that wonderful time when the world is pink and perfect. Normally, this honeymoon phase changes after a while and the relationship settles and becomes a bit calmer. You still feel happy, but the practicalities of life need to be dealt with as well as the romantic aspects. You move from total poetry to a mixture of sometimes poetry and sometimes prose.

However, if you have fallen in love with a narcissist, your relationship will develop in a way you couldn't have dreamt of.

These are the red flags that indicate your romantic partner might be a narcissist.

Overwhelmingly romantic and quick – love bombing

As narcissists are very good at presenting themselves as attentive, loving and lovely for a short period of time, they are keen to make the courting period short and intensive. They will do unbelievably romantic things. From taking you on a surprise flight to have dinner in Paris, putting 100 roses at your front door, sending text messages every hour, to buying you a daily present.

They sweep you off your feet, telling you 'you are the one' and 'how could I have lived without you?' Then they are in a hurry to take the relationship to a different level.

A narcissist's intensive romantic activities are called 'love bombing'. It seems too good to be true. And that is exactly what it is: too good to be true. The purpose of love bombing is to wrap up the partner in the relationship and secure the future.

From Victim to Victor

One lady I spoke to was proposed to within three days after she met her husband-to-be and within six months they were married.

Or the woman who started off in a more or less 'normal' relationship with an attentive narcissist for about one year. However, the moment the couple lived together, the male narcissist changed his tune and became controlling, mean with money and developed rude behaviour.

The fairy tale turned into a nightmare.

> **The intensive romantic activities from the narcissist at the start of the relationship are called 'love bombing'.**
> **It seems too good to be true.**
> **And that is exactly what it is: too good to be true.**
>
> Dr Mariette Jansen

Phrases narcissists use often at the start of a relationship are:

'You're my soul mate.'

'I've never met anyone like you before.'

'You understand me so much better than anyone else.'

'It's fate that we met.'

'I've never felt this way about anyone before.'

'Am I your only friend? You're my only friend.'

'We don't need anyone else.'

'You're so kind, creative, smart, beautiful, and perfect.'

'We'll be together forever.'

The rhythm of hot and cold

Narcissistic partners behave unpredictably. One moment they are warm and loving, next you get the cold shoulder. Maybe it's because you didn't do as they requested, maybe because they want to let you know that you need to deserve their love. It is difficult to predict what you will receive and it is unsettling and undermines your confidence. You start questioning yourself about what you did wrong.

How about the situation where he said you look good in blue? You go out together and you put on a blue dress, to show that you have listened and to please him. The feedback you get is that blue can look good on you, but this blue definitely doesn't.

A client once told me that her partner could be so loving and attentive just before they were going out. And then, without her having any idea what caused it, he would retreat, ignore her and give her the feeling that she had done something wrong. This typical behaviour spoilt a lot of evenings.

Their remarks change from totally loving to critical and devaluing:

'You're crazy.'

'You're too sensitive.'

'No wonder nobody else likes you.'

'My friends hate you, but I always defend you and have your back.'

'You're so insecure.'

'What's wrong with you?'

'Aren't I more important to you than your friends?'

'You're being so manipulative.'

Your partner is incredible

Clever, successful, pretty, powerful and more. You are soooooo lucky to have them. Because how could someone like you entice someone like them… Don't ever forget that. This is one of their power tools.

Life for the narcissist is all about winning. They are often excellent debaters and love a good argument with them emerging as the champion. They also love talking about their area of expertise, which again gives them an opportunity to show off and ensure that you feel small and insignificant.

Any situation or discussion ultimately revolves around them.

If you want to discuss a work topic, they will bring it back to their own work. If you talk about your marathon training, they will start talking about their exercise or non-exercise challenges. The focus of attention needs to be on them. Always.

You are there to offer their Narcissistic Supply. Nothing else.

Total lack of empathy

You will not get the 'oh, poor darling, what a terrible situation for you. It must be so sad, difficult, upsetting…' The reaction you get will be along the lines of dismissiveness, of shrugging shoulders and changing the subject. They simply don't understand emotions and emotional support. A typical remark would be: 'Your tears won't work on me. Why are you crying?'

A particularly painful situation was mentioned by someone who had gone to the funeral of a young cousin. Their narcissistic partner was too busy at work to attend, but not too busy to send a factual text message with a list of shopping items to get on the way home from the funeral.

Moving between hope and fear

Fear of doing something wrong (in your partner's eyes) and being punished via put-downs, being blanked or a change of plans. Where and what you want is not going to happen and sometimes there's even violence.

You hope that it will all pass and that you will return to those feelings that existed when the relationship began.

However, underneath the hope and fear is a belief that you are nothing, and you wouldn't be able to live without your narcissist. The message your partner sends you is around how difficult, demanding and insignificant you are. No one would put up with you, apart from him or her. They instil fear and insecurity in you that prevents you from leaving.

The 'push and pull' which moves you from fear to hope and back is all meant to keep you under control.

They won't let you go

If you have found the courage to leave, they will find the creativity to reel you back in. The glorifying stage will revive. You will forget the reasons why you left this wonderful person, wondering why you are so critical and demanding. Ungrateful even. Your ex will wriggle him or herself back into your life. They will be supportive, help you out, cook dinner, be charming, glorify you. If that doesn't work, they will open the next box of tricks to connect with you, such as sending nice presents, which will push you to respond. Or offering help in a way that would seem rude to refuse... and before you know it, you are back in the relationship you were convinced didn't work for you.

2. The price you pay for the relationship

Healthy love relationships are aimed to make each individual grow, spiritually and emotionally (Scott Peck in *The Road Less Travelled*). Unhealthy relationships use up a lot of emotional and mental energy, just to survive. In the case of a relationship with a narcissist, there are clear losses to be had.

Common prices to be paid:

Loss of confidence

As a result of gaslighting (see checklist point 24), being treated with disrespect and feeling insecure, the partner of a narcissist will lose their confidence, self-esteem and self-worth. Often people don't recognise themselves anymore. 'I never used to be so nervous' and 'I don't recognise myself, I used to be so confident'.

Loss of social interaction and connection with friends and family members

Narcissists disrupt your good relationships. Very often they don't get on with their partner's best friend and don't want them in their house, won't go out as a foursome and really try to alienate their partner from people they get on with. They criticise family members and make family visits an issue.

Loss of money

Often narcissists lie about financial issues and make their partner pay more than their fair share. Or they play the poor victim, so their partner will lend them money or pay their bills.

Loss of independent thinking

After a while, narcissists take up most of their partner's mental space. Their partners tread on eggshells, living in hope and fear, and are continuously anticipating what the narcissist might be thinking, saying or doing. It becomes mental imprisonment.

Loss of freedom

The mental and emotional reprogramming that has been led by the narcissist makes their partner feel powerless. They feel trapped and can't believe there is a way out; instead, holding themselves responsible for choosing their narcissistic partner. 'I made my bed, now I have to lie in it.'

Loss of peace

Life becomes a continuous battle. Being on the lookout for 'danger', by doing the 'wrong' thing in the eyes of the narcissist and getting 'punished' for it. Peace becomes Utopia. Another word for this way of being is hypervigilance, a constant state of high alertness where high levels of several stress hormones are produced. This threatens a person's emotional and physical well-being.

Loss of self

Who am I? What do I think, feel, want? Sometimes the partner becomes so accommodating that they develop strong narcissistic tendencies themselves as well. Often, they lose their values and start to identify with narcissists and become narcissistic themselves. Ultimately, they lose themselves.

> **I have a dream.**
> A dream that will stay a dream forever.
> It is about a baby.
> Just him and me, doing something together.
> Just one more baby that I could hold and love and nurture
> He promised me I could have one, but then he punished me and took the dream away.
> Every month he would bargain: maybe if you have surgery, maybe you lose weight, maybe if we move abroad and each time he would change his mind.
> Just maybe, but the months turned into years... until it was too late.
> The torment over the years was awful.
>
> Another 'take-away' from my narcissistic ex.
>
> A survivor of a narcissistic relationship

3. The Trauma Bond

When someone is under the spell of a narcissist, it seems as if they are addicted, absorbed, chained to them. Their head might tell them to go, but something holds them back. And the longer the relationship lasts, the harder it becomes to end it. What has been formed is a Trauma Bond (Patrick Carnes), which makes it impossible to leave the relationship, no matter how much damage it is doing. The victim believes that the real person is the one who was 'love bombing' and when the mask slips, they think that the new behaviour is out of character and it is their fault that they spark that behaviour. They stay in the relationship because they want to win the affection back.

But also, victims become biologically attached through 'trauma bonding'.

The psychologically abusive relationship is like a rollercoaster, with punishment and intermittent kindness. The body responds to this ongoing situation by continuously producing the stress hormone cortisol, only to be disrupted by the happy hormone dopamine, which flares up when there is kindness. This physical dance between high and low creates an addiction to the dopamine. The only release from the cortisol is the injection of dopamine.

Signs you have developed a Trauma Bond

The checklist below will give you an indication if you have developed a trauma bond with your narcissist.

A constant pattern of broken promises from the narcissist	
People around you are concerned about you in the relationship, but you brush them off	
You feel stuck as you don't see a way out	
The same arguments keep coming up	
You receive regularly punishments for doing something wrong	
You notice physical stress sighs, such as skin conditions, tiredness, headaches, high blood pressure	
An inability to detach from the relationship	
You leave but come back	

4. Ending the relationship

Finishing a relationship with a narcissist is very challenging. If the Trauma Bond is strong, it might feel impossible. And the resistance of the narcissist means they will do anything to make it a nasty process. It is because they feel challenged and rejected, which is unacceptable to them. They are the ones to call the shots, even though they might already be in a new relationship.

To start with, a narcissist will try everything to make a break-up as difficult, expensive and painful as possible. This is particularly challenging when it is a divorce and involves children. The ex-wives are cut off from financial resources and the children are presented with confusing situations. Mum has no money, Dad smothers them in it. Mum tries to organise them, Dad works against her. A very common situation is when the holiday is divided between parents. Mum has an opportunity to take the children with her and spend time with her extended family, which is fun and cheap. Dad will insist he can only take time off during that same period.

In order to prove that this break-up is not because they are not wanted or unpopular, narcissists are usually in another relationship within weeks. Which adds insult to injury and leaves the ex-partner wondering exactly what the value of their relationship was.

Also, 'bad-mouthing' of the ex is very common, such as telling blatant lies that will put the narcissist in a positive light and make people think badly about the ex.

After a while, the narcissist might try to suck the ex-partner back in (hoovering). They will use actions that will bring back the memories of their courting during the first few weeks, which was a fairy tale, and with their smooth talking or their victim attitude, they often succeed in luring their ex back in. There are cases where this has happened several times. The best break-up scenario is to cut it off clean and never be in touch again. However, with a shared history, children, financial commitments and an emotional investment, this might seem impossible.

The main legacy of the relationship will be confusion. Confusion about what happened, what was real, what wasn't, and it is that confusion that plays into the hands of a narcissist.

Hoovering

Hoovering refers to sucking you back in, like a vacuum cleaner or a hoover does, and is attributed to narcissism. A narcissist wants to be part of a romantic and family relationship as they need to manipulate people to get their Narcissistic Supply. Being left by their partner feels like a rejection, which feeds their insecurity and it makes them really angry. It hits their weak spot of not being good enough and 'who do you think you are to not want me?' Everyone who I have spoken to struggled with breaking free. From romantic partners to family members. After the initial separation, a narcissist puts a lot of effort into re-establishing the relationship.

You are dealing with an addict who needs their fix, the Narcissistic Supply, and as you were a good supplier, they don't want to let you go.

Hoovering entails actions such as begging, seducing, guilt-tripping, yelling, shaming, making false accusations, playing the victim, being needy, talking badly about you and more. Most hoovering actions are aimed to provoke a reaction and once that reaction has been given, there will be new ammunition for the narcissist to continue the communication and ultimately get you back.

They only want you back to prove that they are good enough, to punish you for rejecting them and to take back full control over you.

There are several ways to get you back on board.

Presents

After a son decided to not be in touch with his parents, he was inundated with expensive presents sent to his home. This was a clever tactic of those parents, aimed to wriggle themselves back in. Their son had to make a decision and during that process, he was thinking about them. They were back in his mind. Most people think there are two options to respond. Not wanting to be rude means sending a 'thank you' message. Which is engagement. Or alternatively, choosing to send the presents back, which is also a form of engagement. The third option is the preferred one: no response at all and throwing the present away or handing it to a charity shop. In keeping the present, you also invite the 'presence' of the giver in your mental and emotional space.

Poor me

Even if a person leaves a narcissist, there is usually still a soft empathy spot inside and the narcissist will press that button by playing the 'poor me' card. They might be ill, struck by disaster or in big trouble and really need your help… As they have no issue with lying, the 'poor me' is easily made up by the narcissist. There are examples of people who even faked cancer or a heart attack.

Apologies

As a means of hoovering, a narcissist might write a letter of apology saying that they didn't mean what they did, they are so sorry and can you forgive them? They are full of remorse and good intentions and it is an effective way to reign people back in.

Flying monkeys

Flying monkeys (see Checklist point 10) are the allies of narcissists. They have been reeled in via stories about your bad behaviour and how you have upset the narcissist. The flying monkeys spread gossip and rumours about you, get in touch with you as a hoovering tool and generally advocate on behalf of narcissists. They make narcissists feel important and grandiose.

How to deal with hoovering?

1. Once you have decided to move away from a narcissist, stick to it.
2. Do not engage with any of their hoovering actions.
3. Ignore them, even if they start using other people to get in touch (flying monkeys).
4. Your relationship with a narcissist is a closed book. Keep that book closed forever.

It is very difficult to leave a narcissist behind. And there is a lot of intelligence in the way they try to hoover you up again. Be aware!

Part III:
The Narcissist Checklist

Introduction

In this part of the book, I present you with the checklist I have put together. It is a tool for you to see what the typical behaviour of a narcissist (or suspected narcissist) is. The devil is in the detail. Having an insight into a narcissist's specific behaviour will help you to find responses that will damage you less or protect you. This checklist will help you get a grip and an understanding of events that cause confusion or undermine confidence.

I have spoken to hundreds of people who scored their narcissist and all came up with at least 40 of the 50 traits.

The checklist presents typical traits and behaviours. It is not a clinical diagnostic tool. It is a practical tool for suspected victims of narcissistic abuse.

It will help to distinguish the narcissist from the cocky self-absorbed salesperson; the annoying, controlling organizer; or the clever, ambitious and arrogant scientist.

1. How to use the checklist

People are unique. They all have their own combination of traits. With this checklist, it is possible to determine if you have a narcissist in your life, their specific habits and how you are affected. Once you recognise them, you can start developing the most effective responses to their behaviour.

Remember, we all behave badly from time to time. That doesn't make us all narcissists. It is the number of traits and the fact that narcissists try to cover their tracks and hide their true behaviour which is a good indicator of the level of narcissism.

Step 1

Go through the checklist and mark each point from a factual perspective. If you are not sure what is meant, read the more detailed description with examples (further in this chapter) before you give your answer. There is only one option: yes or no. 'Not all the time' is a yes, 'sometimes' is a yes, 'never saw it' is a no. Be clear and firm.

- If you notice yourself making excuses for some of the traits (only when they are tired, stressed, busy, etc.),
- If you are talking the points down as 'not too important' or 'you don't mind it',
- If you think they 'don't mean it',

it is a 'yes'.

Step 2

Go through the more detailed description of the traits and add your personal example(s). This brings the checklist to life and will help you to recognise different situations.

Step 3

Answer the following questions for each box you ticked:

a. How does this affect my happiness? (0-10)

0 = it doesn't contribute to my happiness at all
10 = it makes me very happy

b. How does this affect my stress levels? (0-10)

0 = it doesn't give me any stress
10 = it completely stresses me out

c. How strongly am I in control? (0-10)

1 = I am not in control at all
10 = I feel totally in control

d. How do I react to this situation/trait?
- *What do I feel?*
- *What do I think?*
- *How do I behave?*

This is quite a task, but it will make clear how strong or weak the influence of your narcissist is on your happiness and well-being.

There is a separate workbook available via Amazon, which contains all the worksheets, which are referring to the checklist.

The Narcissist Checklist

Mark each characteristic that applies.

My narcissist:

1	**Category I** **Has a grandiose view of self-importance**
2	Values status, money, class, education, clothes to enhance self or family image
3	Chooses a partner they can easily control
4	Is better, more successful, brilliant, beautiful or powerful than others
5	Has a high opinion of themselves, is 'special' and tries to mingle with other 'special' people
6	Demands excessive admiration
7	Shows arrogant, rude and abusive behaviour in private situations
8	Doesn't give genuine compliments
9	Is the centre of the universe and aims to be the centre of others' universe as well
10	Has recruited an army of flying monkeys
11	**Category II** **Has a sense of entitlement**
12	Is beyond the law
13	Will not thank or appreciate others
14	Expects to be obeyed and served
15	Expects the best without putting in an effort
16	Is envious
17	Loves spending money on themselves
18	Dictates and sets the rules
19	Has double standards
20	**Category III** **Will control and manipulate**
21	Acts differently in public than in private
22	Will lie to suit their agenda

23	Reframes situations
24	Is good at gaslighting
25	Is unreliable
26	Divides and rules
27	Alienates family members and friends
28	Uses money and presents as power tools
29	A parent chooses roles: golden child, scapegoat and the invisible one
30	Is secretive about their finances
31	Is good at emotional blackmail
32	Plays the victim
33	Is exploitative
34	Is skilful at masking their narcissism
35	**Category IV** **Can't handle any form of criticism**
36	Doesn't take ownership or responsibility when things go wrong
37	Gets angry about contrary viewpoints
38	Is keen to point out what is wrong in others
39	Is highly reactive to criticism
40	Considers every situation in the light of winning
41	**Category V** **Lacks empathy and emotional awareness**
42	Laughs at other's misfortune – Schadenfreude
43	Takes everything literally
44	Thinks in black and white
45	Is suspicious
46	Can be very cruel
47	Can't discuss emotional issues
48	Is not interested in other people
49	Has no self-awareness
50	Is emotionally distant and unavailable

The different traits fall into one of the five categories that define a narcissist. If someone shows a lot of traits in a certain category, it will help you to find the most helpful responses.

It is not always clear-cut to which category a trait belongs. But as this is a tool to help to indicate and recognise and not to clinically diagnose, it will work regardless.

2. CATEGORY I:
Grandiose view of self-importance

Narcissists are convinced that they are fabulous, interesting and top-dog. They have a distorted view of their importance and their value. It is their biggest protection mechanism and serves to hide their fragile ego. If they were to look at themselves through the eyes of others, they would crumble. Their insecurity would come to the surface and they would be seen for who they really are. This is like death to the narcissist and needs to be avoided at all costs.

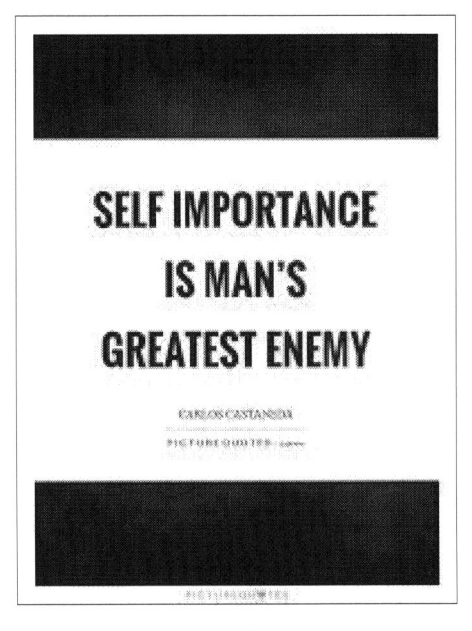

SELF IMPORTANCE IS MAN'S GREATEST ENEMY

CARLOS CASTANEDA

1. My narcissist has a grandiose view of self-importance

If you think you are the centre of the universe, the sun shines out of your bottom and you are the best thing since sliced bread, you believe you can get away with a lot of things that others can't. A true narcissist will also make clear that they should be the centre of your universe and that manifests itself in seeking attention.

When they are in a group, they will always divert attention to themselves. If someone tells a story, they might talk over them or have a better story to tell. They will do anything to be the centrepiece. After all, in their opinion, everybody is there to pay attention to them by listening, pleasing and helping, and it should be an honour to do so.

How would this trait manifest itself?

My mother

The starting point of each family decision would revolve around her.

- Where shall we go on holiday? Wherever she wants to go.
- What do we eat at Christmas? Whatever she chooses.

She hated funerals and weddings because it was impossible for her to be the centre of attention at those occasions. She loved to make scenes at social family get-togethers where we celebrated someone else's happy moments. The drama she created would make her the central person, which was just what she aimed for.

The romantic partner

Same principle. Joint decisions don't happen. It is always the narcissist's one that counts and yours are dismissed. You are not important, they are. In day-to-day life, they expect their partner to do jobs for them, bail them out and literally serve them. Their partner becomes quite subservient and manages their life together around the wishes of the narcissist.

It is expected that the partner supports the narcissist's wishes about social and family activities. They like to avoid events where it would be difficult for them to shine such as get-togethers with the partner's family. Of course, they expect their partner to stay with them and not attend those events.

Other examples

'My husband refuses to wait anywhere. He won't queue in a shop or at the bank. He will just bash forwards and charmingly say to people that he is in a hurry. When he has no choice, like at the check-in desk at an airport, he is fuming.' Waiting their turn is a huge challenge for the narcissist as it doesn't show them as the special being they think they are.

This is how my narcissist presents this trait:

How does this affect my happiness? (0-10)
How does this affect my stress levels? (0-10)
How strongly am I in control? (0-10)

How do I react to this situation/trait?

What do I feel?

What do I think?

How do I behave?

Notes

2. My narcissist values status, money, class, education, clothes to enhance self or family image

External presentation is very important to the narcissist. After all, there is no internal substance, no self-awareness and no self-love. All narcissists work on their image, but they have their personal preferences depending on their personal backgrounds.

My mother

Coming from a family with lots of money, she considered herself as belonging to a higher class. Table manners, and all that went with it, were important to her as well as laying out the table with silver cutlery, a separate silver jam jar with a silver spoon, special grape scissors and other old-fashioned but chic items. Even though none of the rest of the family paid attention to that.

The romantic partner

A narcissistic partner might impress with expensive presents, which are visible to others and will show that they have money. One lady received a brand-new car that was presented to her during a party, so everyone was aware of the gift.

An intimate exchange of presents is not the narcissists type of thing. What is the point if they can't show off to a bigger audience?

Other examples

Going to the theatre or a museum, not because they enjoy it but because it gives them the status of being culturally developed and interesting. Same with posh holiday destinations, designer clothes and so on.

This is how my narcissist presents this trait:

How does this affect my happiness? (0-10)
How does this affect my stress levels? (0-10)
How strongly am I in control? (0-10)
How do I react to this situation/trait?
What do I feel?

What do I think?

How do I behave?

Notes

3. My narcissist has chosen a partner they can easily control

The narcissist needs to build their fortress with people they can rely on. They require unconditional support, regular Narcissistic Supply and no criticism. The best person for their safe haven is their spouse. Narcissists have a sixth sense at spotting the people who are overly empathic. The courting phase is aimed at checking them out and one of the tools they use is 'love bombing'. Love bombing takes place at the start of the relationship and is a sequence of amazing experiences to show the potential partner that they deserve only the best.

However, love bombing is all about 'magic' and not about realness. Not about getting to know each other, but about being wrapped up in a fantasy. Soon after the love bombing, narcissists want to take a relationship to the next level: living together, even marriage. They can't keep up appearances for too long and are in a hurry to secure their prize.

My mother

My parents got married within a year of meeting each other. My father doted on her. He thought she was so sweet and soft and caring. As he had no other experience with a romantic relationship, he was an easy prey. She always got her way, he only spoke after she nudged him with approval and he never spoke about 'I' and 'me', always 'we' and 'us'.

The romantic partner

Many stories have a fairy tale start and a nightmare ending. 'My husband was such a charmer and he seemed so attentive and generous. I wasn't used to that and it felt very, very special. That all changed after he had proposed. It seemed I was with a different person. He reminded me regularly of the fun we had at the start, telling me that I was so different then. I couldn't get my head around it. And in order to keep the peace, I did anything to please him.'

Other examples

'I had a friendship with another girl for a few years and it was interesting to see how it all changed. In the beginning, we talked a lot and it was easy to tell her my life story. We got on so well. I thought. But then I noticed that she always wanted to have her way: she chose the film, the theatre, when and where to meet. It felt like an unbalanced friendship and I didn't want to have her as a friend anymore.'

> The three biggest lies:
> I am what I have
> I am what I do
> I am what people say about me.
>
> Author not known

This is how my narcissist presents this trait:

....
....
....
....

How does this affect my happiness? (0-10) ....
How does this affect my stress levels? (0-10) ....
How strongly am I in control? (0-10) ....

How do I react to this situation/trait?

What do I feel?

....
....
....

What do I think?

....
....
....

How do I behave?

....
....
....

Notes

....
....
....
....
....

4. My narcissist is better, more successful, brilliant, beautiful or powerful than others

Narcissists believe themselves to be more successful, brilliant, beautiful and powerful than anybody else. Their experiences are more exciting, their homes more beautiful, their children are better educated, more intelligent, and the list goes on. They have a strong competitive edge and they will always be top dog.

My mother

Just after my sister died, she phoned me and she shouted at me: 'It is much harder to lose a daughter than a sister….' I had to be compassionate towards her as my loss was nothing compared to hers.

Her brother and his wife had bought a brand-new very trendy and very expensive retirement apartment on the waterfront. My mother commented that it didn't have a garden like hers and wasn't next to the shops, like hers. In other words, she was better off. Note that they lived in a manky house, where everything was falling apart.

The romantic partner

You might have a better job, but they will say that their career prospects are so much better.

You might have a large social circle, but they will tell you that their friends are so much more interesting than yours.

There is no equality in the relationship and there never will be.

Other examples

'I started to run, doing the Couch to 5K programme and whenever I tell my brother how far I ran, he tells me he has done three half marathons.' He always outperforms me and will never compliment me on my achievements.

This is how my narcissist presents this trait:

How does this affect my happiness? (0-10)
How does this affect my stress levels? (0-10)
How strongly am I in control? (0-10)

How do I react to this situation/trait?

What do I feel?

What do I think?

How do I behave?

Notes

5. My narcissist has a high opinion of themselves, is 'special' and looks to mingle with other 'special' people

Narcissists look up to celebrities, highly educated, very successful or very rich people and they seek to mingle with them in order to be confirmed in their own specialness. They love to throw names around, tell stories as if they were in them and thrive on derived admiration. They look to join the high-end golf clubs, gyms and other places in the hopes of meeting the 'high and mighty'. Wherever they are, they want to be seen with the leaders.

My mother

My mother loved highly-educated people and medical consultants. When she met a lady at tennis, she discovered that her husband was a gynaecologist. She then introduced the lady as 'This is Linda. Her husband is a gynaecologist.'

Tennis was deemed very posh in those days in The Netherlands. My mother was one of the few ladies to play it and she was a member at two clubs.

She went to a different town to a very 'chique' shop to buy clothes and she was probably also one of the first people who had a personal assistant.

My parents' first skiing holiday, in the days when skiing was not a commodity, was in Davos, the jet-set resort.

The romantic partner

'At a party, she always scans the room and then heads towards the people she thinks are interesting to her. You know, the guy with the trendy suit or the advertising director.... And I don't see her again until we go home. I then get a story full of details about someone fantastic she met. It makes me feel crap about myself.'

Other examples

The guy sees himself as part of the jet-set and he chooses his holiday destinations accordingly. His destinations are St Tropez, Capri and Hawaii. Even though he hardly has the money to afford it, he will still go for the fix of being surrounded by famous, important and rich people. And of course, being able to brag about it.

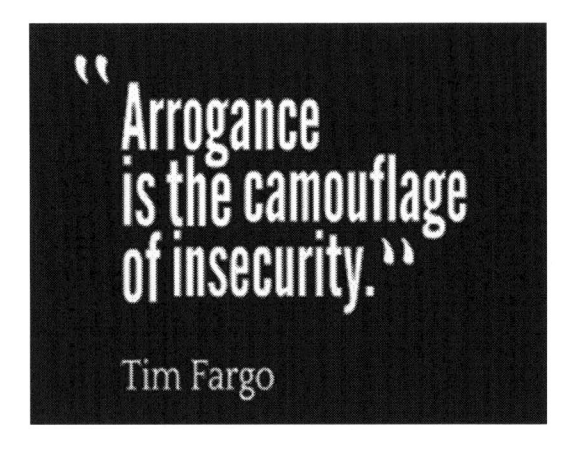

> "Arrogance is the camouflage of insecurity."
>
> Tim Fargo

This is how my narcissist presents this trait:

....
....
....
....

How does this affect my happiness? (0-10) ....
How does this affect my stress levels? (0-10) ....
How strongly am I in control? (0-10) ....

How do I react to this situation/trait?

What do I feel?

....
....
....

What do I think?

....
....
....

How do I behave?

....
....
....

Notes

....
....
....
....

6. My narcissist demands excessive admiration

Narcissists are like addicts, needing their ongoing fix: Narcissistic Supply. They hide their vulnerable and insecure ego, but NS builds them up and makes them feel good through attention and admiration. People around narcissists are expected to compliment and admire them. If it doesn't happen spontaneously, they are manipulated into doing so. Alternatively, narcissists give themselves compliments and pretend they have been given by somebody else.

My mother

Every day, we children, were expected to compliment my mother about the meal she cooked. She wasn't a good or creative cook and her food was rather boring, but there was no way we could voice that. Then we had to compliment her about her clothes, her looks, how good a tennis player she was, and more. On my wedding day, my father told me I looked wonderful. My mother looked at him and he hastily added, 'Nearly as beautiful as your mother on our wedding day'.

The romantic partner

A narcissist will ask daily what their partner thinks of their hair, their muscular torso or their general looks.

Other examples

Someone singing their own praises in a question format, such as, 'Who in the room here has done a marathon?' – ME – or 'Remind me who has excellent history knowledge?' – ME.

The person who keeps on telling everyone what a demanding and important job they are doing. They only stop talking about it when everyone has told them how fantastic they are and give them confirmation.

This is how my narcissist presents this trait:

How does this affect my happiness? (0-10)
How does this affect my stress levels? (0-10)
How strongly am I in control? (0-10)

How do I react to this situation/trait?

What do I feel?

What do I think?

How do I behave?

Notes

7. My narcissist shows arrogant, rude and abusive behaviour in private situations

If they feel like it, they just behave with arrogance and rudeness. They know they will get away with it and usually they don't care. Especially at home.

My mother

My mother had no issue with letting other people wait. As she was the queen, she always made an entrance as a queen. When guests arrived at our house, she was never there, but emerged ten minutes later, perfectly dressed, floating down the stairs while everybody stood waiting for her.

The romantic partner

A narcissist is known for showing their true colours after the love bombing period. Behaviour includes not being interested, dismissive and throwing put-downs around like confetti. When one partner, a nurse, came home after a traumatic day at work in the hospital and wanted to talk about it, her narcissist answered: 'I think you are just not capable of doing your job properly. And what type of job is it anyway… Anyone with low intellect could do it better than you.'

Other examples

There is this story of the gentleman who always complained. On holiday, he wanted to upgrade his room; in a restaurant, he sent back his food; if he received a present, it was definitely not the right thing. He didn't communicate this gently and elegantly. He barked, used aggressive language and embarrassed the people around him.

This is how my narcissist presents this trait:

How does this affect my happiness? (0-10)
How does this affect my stress levels? (0-10)
How strongly am I in control? (0-10)

How do I react to this situation/trait?

What do I feel?

What do I think?

How do I behave?

Notes

8. My narcissist doesn't give genuine compliments

Compliments make other people look good and it might mean they outshine the narcissist. The only comment that can come close to a compliment would be if they admit that someone is doing nearly as well as they are or they put a sting in it…

My mother

I remember a visiting acquaintance of my parents, telling me that I was so creative and how wonderful that was. I had never heard that before, but it struck me and stayed with me. I received a genuine compliment and that was a new experience. It felt great. But I also remember how dismissive my mother looked.

She would say how I was a reasonable tennis player, and that I got that from her. So, indirectly she gave herself that compliment.

The romantic partner

One lady mentioned how her husband kept on telling her for years that 'she was a great mother but a crap wife'. The one good thing was immediately cancelled out by the bad thing.

Other examples

It is all about compliments that hold a sting. Like 'You wear really nice trousers; they make you look less fat.'

'New hairdresser? This style suits you so much better than the old one.'

The Narcissist Checklist

This is how my narcissist presents this trait:

....
....
....
....

How does this affect my happiness? (0-10) ....
How does this affect my stress levels? (0-10) ....
How strongly am I in control? (0-10) ....

How do I react to this situation/trait?

What do I feel?

....
....
....

What do I think?

....
....
....

How do I behave?

....
....
....

Notes

....
....
....
....

9. My narcissist is the centre of the universe and aims to be the centre of others' universe as well

The self-orientation of the narcissist is clear. Every situation and event is about them. They are like children. And through their manipulation techniques, they try to make themselves the centre of your universe as well. They want you to focus on them more than on yourself.

My mother

If I didn't put her on a pedestal, I was dismissed, ignored, looked down on and she made me feel unworthy. However, my worth was restored when I adhered to what she wanted and needed; and as a young person I often gave in.

The romantic partner

The relationship is about the partner and they claim their space in the other person's life through ensuring that a lot of attention and thought is given to them. One lady who was going through a divorce came to realise that for the last 20 years, she had been constantly thinking of her partner. What did he want for dinner? Where did he want to go on holiday? What did he want to watch on TV? What did he think, why did he do that, will this action change him? It was a big revelation to discover how much mental energy she gave away to him.

Other examples

In a friendship group, narcissists manipulate the group in such a way that they always get what they want. They decide where to go for dinner, the film to watch and where to drink. They make the choices and decisions. A description of the 'dominant bully' springs to mind.

This is how my narcissist presents this trait:

....

....

....

How does this affect my happiness? (0-10) ....

How does this affect my stress levels? (0-10) ....

How strongly am I in control? (0-10) ....

How do I react to this situation/trait?

What do I feel?

....

....

What do I think?

....

....

How do I behave?

....

....

Notes

....

....

....

....

10. My narcissist has recruited an army of flying monkeys

Narcissists 'collect' people around them who will be supportive and act on their behalf, usually for abusive purposes. A smear campaign needs an audience and the flying monkeys will take on board what they hear from the narcissist as the truth. The victim is the nasty person, the 'bad guy', and the narcissist needs to be protected. The flying monkeys are also there to spy on behalf of the narcissist and if need be, to punish you.

Families are a great source for flying monkeys and aunts, cousins and far-away family members will be vetted for their suitability as flying monkeys.

Flying monkeys are also asked to be active in the hoovering process.

My mother

People who were employed by my parents were all sucked into the flying monkey roles. They heard the stories of the horrible things I did to my 'innocent' parents. I received phone calls, emails and even letters, trying to seduce me into being in contact again.

During the funeral of my brother most family members turned their back on me and didn't speak to me. I thought that was strange, but later on, I understood that they were infected with the toxic stories of my cruelty. And were recruited into the army.

The romantic partner

Narcissists tell friends about how concerned they are about the mental well-being of their partner – their lately unusual, aggressive behaviour. Could the friends please keep an eye out and report back anything that is going on?

The friends think how nice and loving the narcissist is, but they couldn't see that they have been set up to not take their own friend seriously. Would they belief it, if there were complaints about the lovely narcissist? Unknowingly to them, they were lured into the army of the flying monkeys.

Other examples

Ganging up to spy on social media on behalf of a narcissist and helping them to get more ammunition to harm their victim.

> Narcissists recruit their army.
> Then they instruct and sit back,
> waiting for the results.
> If the results are what they want,
> They take the credits.
> If the results are not what they want,
> they blame their monkeys.
> And humiliate them.
>
> Dr Mariette Jansen

This is how my narcissist presents this trait:

How does this affect my happiness? (0-10)
How does this affect my stress levels? (0-10)
How strongly am I in control? (0-10)

How do I react to this situation/trait?

What do I feel?

What do I think?

How do I behave?

Notes

3. CATEGORY II:
Has a sense of entitlement

Narcissists believe they are a special breed, who deserve special treatment and privileges. Just because they are who they are. They have the rights without them doing anything to 'deserve' it. This translates into unreasonable expectations and demands. But they also have a lazy approach to life. Things are supposed to come to them. Just because…

'I deserve' (unearned privileges) is the mental attitude overwriting the healthy attitude of 'I am responsible' (for getting what I want/need).

'Entitlement is a delusion built on self-centeredness and laziness'

Author not known

11. My narcissist has a sense of entitlement

Narcissists have a sense of entitlement, where they are convinced they deserve certain privileges and are arrogant about it.

My mother

My mother was entitled to her daily breakfast in bed, a new wardrobe each season and her skiing holidays. She didn't appreciate those things as special. I guess, as she considered herself as special, she considered them to be a normal consequence.

The romantic partner

Several partners have experienced how their narcissist approached sex as an entitlement. And when they didn't get what they wanted, they got it elsewhere. Lots of narcissists have affairs. Justifying it with: 'If you don't give me what I need, I have to get it from someone else.' And they usually add a put-down to it: 'It was really great sex. The best I have had in ages.'

Other examples

The mother in law who wouldn't dream of arranging her own travel by train or taxi, but feels she should be chauffeured to any family gathering and driven home afterwards.

This is how my narcissist presents this trait:

How does this affect my happiness? (0-10)
How does this affect my stress levels? (0-10)
How strongly am I in control? (0-10)

How do I react to this situation/trait?

What do I feel?

What do I think?

How do I behave?

Notes

12. My narcissist is beyond the law

The law is for normal people, not for elevated beings. A narcissist has no problem ignoring the rules, even if they have been pointed out explicitly. Narcissists lack an internal warning system, which kicks in place when you do something wrong. A little voice called your conscience.

My mother

She had no problem parking in a disabled space or spaces allocated to others.

She also loved to leave a shop with goods she hadn't paid for. Often pretended it was an accident. She also never pointed out when the cashier made a mistake in her favour.

The romantic partner

What happens inside the house, should stay inside, which means that all sorts of abuse can take place without it being acknowledged as wrong. Physical violence is not unusual in a narcissistic relationship. Sometimes it is the victim that lashes out, from pure frustration and anger. One lady was appalled by her behaviour: 'I was throwing my phone at him, just to stop him shouting at me. And that is so against how I want to behave but it just happened. As if I was going mad…'

Other examples

During Covid-19 the narcissist continued to have 'family' BBQs with friends and family from different places at a time when the public was asked to socially distance and stay at home as much as possible.

This is how my narcissist presents this trait:

_____
_____
_____
_____

How does this affect my happiness? (0-10) _____
How does this affect my stress levels? (0-10) _____
How strongly am I in control? (0-10) _____

How do I react to this situation/trait?

What do I feel?

_____
_____
_____

What do I think?

_____
_____
_____

How do I behave?

_____
_____
_____

Notes

_____
_____
_____
_____

13. My narcissist will not thank or appreciate others

Narcissists believe the world is organised to serve them. Everyone is seen as a 'servant' and servants just have to do their job and don't need a thank you.

My mother

I had two sons, her grandsons. I regularly sent some photos as I knew she would like that. Then at one stage, I stopped as I never got an acknowledgement or thank you. She then moaned that I had stopped sending photos and I told her that there must have been trouble at the post office because I had sent regularly. They apparently never arrived as I never heard anything.

The romantic partner

When a partner arranges an exclusive weekend away, narcissists accept it at face value and never mention it again.

Other examples

The narcissistic friend asks favours of you and expects you to just do them.

This is how my narcissist presents this trait:

....

....

....

....

How does this affect my happiness? (0-10) ....

How does this affect my stress levels? (0-10) ....

How strongly am I in control? (0-10) ....

How do I react to this situation/trait?

What do I feel?

....

....

....

What do I think?

....

....

....

How do I behave?

....

....

....

Notes

....

....

....

....

14. My narcissist expects to be obeyed and served

My wish is your command. Don't expect to get away with not doing what they have told you to do. These are not requests with the option to say no. These are orders.

My mother

At the slightest hint of what she wanted, my father set off into a frenzy to run around and make it happen.

My mother spent a lot of time in her music room. I guess it was the equivalent of a boudoir. When I came home, I had to go upstairs and meet and greet her in her music room with a kiss. She also demanded a kiss whenever I left.

The romantic partner

One woman said her husband would tell her every morning what he wanted for dinner and more obscurely, what he wanted her to wear. This tied in with his sexual entitlement.

Other examples

There was the mother who had her son's rota on the fridge so she knew when he was off work and planned all sorts of chores for him to do.

The gentleman narcissist brought his car to the garage and expected to be served immediately. The mechanic told him he was fully booked for the next two days. The gentleman shouted: 'Do you know who I am?' The mechanic shrugged his shoulders. Clearly not and he wasn't interested either. The gentleman left to find another garage.

This is how my narcissist presents this trait:

How does this affect my happiness? (0-10)
How does this affect my stress levels? (0-10)
How strongly am I in control? (0-10)

How do I react to this situation/trait?

What do I feel?

What do I think?

How do I behave?

Notes

15. My narcissist expects the best without putting in any effort

A narcissist's grandiose idea about themselves goes with the default belief that they are the best. Naturally. Whereas normal people understand they might need to work to achieve something, narcissists are lazy.

My mother

My mother spent most of her days on her lounging chair in the garden, sunbathing. She would happily sit with her fur coat on in the chair with her face catching the sunrays on cold but sunny days. It is a bit surreal, thinking about that obsession and how everyone accepted that that was just what she was doing. She never put in any effort for anything.

When she was about 80, we had another argument, and she said with a voice full of drama: 'I had expected my retirement to be very different.' I remember thinking, 'retirement from what?' and 'you will reap what you sow'.

The romantic partner

At dinner parties, narcissists shine and accept compliments about the preparation and work done by their partner, who slaved the whole day in the kitchen.

Other examples

Narcissists will use and manipulate anyone around them to get the best. They believe they are too good to make an effort as long as others can do it for them.

They will always tag along to any event that someone else has organised.

Be aware at work, where a narcissistic colleague or boss will take compliments and rewards for work that is done by others.

This is how my narcissist presents this trait:

How does this affect my happiness? (0-10)
How does this affect my stress levels? (0-10)
How strongly am I in control? (0-10)

How do I react to this situation/trait?

What do I feel?

What do I think?

How do I behave?

Notes

16. My narcissist is envious

Narcissists can't accept that someone else should have more and be better. They will try to take away the shine from another person. If it can't be the narcissist, it definitely can't be someone else either. Narcissists are always comparing notes with others and when others seem to be in a better position, it sparks their jealousy. 'I want what you have. And if I can't have it, I will make sure that you can't have it either.' For them, it would be a recognition that they are less than someone else. They are also very skilful at twisting a situation to point out how they are the victim of someone else's jealousy.

My mother

My mother told us children time and again that there was no better husband than my father. It would be impossible to find someone like him. She had the best.

Once she told me that my then-boyfriend was a no-hoper and not a patch on her husband. I told her I didn't fancy the type of relationship my parents had and she laughed, saying I was just jealous.

Whenever I had some really nice clothes that got me compliments from others, she would ruin them in the wash.

The romantic partner

One partner of a narcissist came from a huge family: three siblings, lots of uncles and aunts, endless cousins and nieces. There was often an informal family get-together as they all got on and loved spending time with each other. The narcissist boasted that they were so lucky to just be the two of them and that her family really envied them for the freedom they had and the option to spend time together.

Other examples

Narcissists might gossip about others and make up stories about how they have been mistreated by them, attempting to put the people they are jealous of in a bad light.

> I always deserve the best.
> If you have the best,
> I want it.
> And if I can't have what you have,
> I will make sure
> That you can't have it either.
>
> Dr Mariette Jansen

This is how my narcissist presents this trait:

How does this affect my happiness? (0-10)
How does this affect my stress levels? (0-10)
How strongly am I in control? (0-10)

How do I react to this situation/trait?

What do I feel?

What do I think?

How do I behave?

Notes

17. My narcissist loves spending money on themselves

Narcissists know that the best way to spend money is to spend it on themselves. Why would they give it to others? The only way it makes sense to spend on others is when it is about showing off, because it then rubs off positively onto them.

My mother

Now a mother myself, I notice how often I give my sons a little extra money. Just for fun or because they want to buy something or because I had a very good month in my business. It is the joy of sharing and making them happy. This is something my mother never did.

On the contrary, she kept on asking for money. When we were invited to dinner, there would always be a money catch, which meant we had to pay.

The romantic partner

Often narcissists withhold money and don't pay for joint bills. Or they claim they've left their wallet behind, lost a card and can't pay. This is a general pattern where narcissists focus on growing their private pots at the expense of their partners'.

Narcissists buy designer clothes for themselves but shop with their partners at department stores for regular suits and basic casual clothes.

Other examples

There are lots of stories around the inconsistent messages of not having enough money, but always enough for a holiday, a facial or some other extravaganza.

This is how my narcissist presents this trait:

....
....
....
....

How does this affect my happiness? (0-10) ....
How does this affect my stress levels? (0-10) ....
How strongly am I in control? (0-10) ....

How do I react to this situation/trait?

What do I feel?

....
....
....

What do I think?

....
....
....

How do I behave?

....
....
....

Notes

....
....
....
....

18. My narcissist dictates and sets the rules

Life needs to be controlled by the narcissist. They set the scene and everyone must follow their dictatorship.

My mother

She controlled everybody and everything in our home. Having a sleep-in was not accepted and she would bounce on my bedroom door at 8.30 on a Saturday or Sunday morning. She forced me to drink warm milk, which made me gag. She sent me and my brother each Saturday afternoon to the swimming pool until I was about 16. There was no discussion, it all happened as she wanted.

The romantic relationship

Life will go according to their plans and planning. One lady, who loved to exercise, had negotiated two hours of exercise each weekend – one gym session and one run. Even though her narcissistic husband and father of their two children had agreed, he changed their plans often and didn't respect their agreement. Instead of exercising the woman had to look after her children. This always happened when she had done something 'wrong' and he thought she needed to be punished.

Other examples

In friendship groups, narcissists make sure they get their way. Watch out for the bully and the big shouter.

This is how my narcissist presents this trait:

....
....
....
....

How does this affect my happiness? (0-10) ....

How does this affect my stress levels? (0-10) ....

How strongly am I in control? (0-10) ....

How do I react to this situation/trait?

What do I feel?

....
....
....

What do I think?

....
....
....

How do I behave?

....
....
....

Notes

....
....
....
....

19. My narcissist has double standards

Different situations are judged differently. Narcissists will tell someone off for behaviour they apply themselves.

> He smiled when she said: 'Happy birthday darling.'
> He waited a minute and said with a sharp voice: 'Where is my birthday present?'
> She nearly choked and answered with a trembling voice: 'But we agreed to not do presents anymore.'
> He snarled: 'Stupid cow. You never understand what I say. I meant not for you. It doesn't apply to me.'
> And he left the house in a strop.
> She burst into tears and had no idea when he would be back.
> Not a happy birthday for her.
>
> From a victim of narcissistic abuse

My mother

She was always complaining that people didn't send thank you notes. She never ever wrote one herself.

She was always very opinionated about women over 60 who were still playing tennis. 'Ridiculous, to run around in a tennis dress with those old legs... They should have stopped years ago.' She kept on playing way into her seventies. But, if you pointed that out to her, you were in trouble.

The romantic partner

Narcissists expect birthday cards, presents and balloons for their birthday, but never give them to their partner.

Other examples

Being annoyed when someone is constantly on their phone while being on theirs all the time.

This is how my narcissist presents this trait:

How does this affect my happiness? (0-10)
How does this affect my stress levels? (0-10)
How strongly am I in control? (0-10)

How do I react to this situation/trait?

What do I feel?

What do I think?

How do I behave?

Notes

4. CATEGORY III:
Will control and manipulate

Narcissists are extremely manipulative and ensure that people around them think and act the way they want. They apply a number of different techniques to deceive the people around them. They don't see the damage they are doing and are only focused on and interested in what they get out of it.

The need for control has everything to do with their need to feel safe and trust that their fragile ego is protected.

The Narcissist Checklist

> People who feel the need to control others, don't have control over themselves.

20. My narcissist will control

The hunger for control is born out of insecurity and narcissists have plenty of that. They mask their fragile, insecure egos and make sure they get enough Narcissistic Supply to feed their grandiosity and feel okay.

It is difficult for a narcissist to relax and go with the flow. Nor knowing is scary and makes them vulnerable. Therefore, they aim to take control of people and situations, using a range of manipulative techniques.

My mother

She never let my father do his own thing without her being there. When he started his little choir, she started running and ran to where he was rehearsing and sat at the back of the room. Observing.

The romantic partner

There is not a lot of space for personal actions when living with a narcissist. 'Where are you off to?' 'Why are you doing it like that? You should do it like this.' 'Who are you talking to?' An endless list of enquiries with commentary. Tiring. But also, there is not a lot of space to just be by yourself and be yourself.

Other examples

One way of getting control is knowledge. The narcissist will bombard you with questions to get to know you or the situation and then have the ammunition to control you.

A lot of narcissists have a habit of taking a position, from a doorway, a chair, a corner and then stare at their victim, who usually feels very uncomfortable and confused.

This is how my narcissist presents this trait:

How does this affect my happiness? (0-10)
How does this affect my stress levels? (0-10)
How strongly am I in control? (0-10)

How do I react to this situation/trait?

What do I feel?

What do I think?

How do I behave?

Notes

21. My narcissist acts differently in public than in private

Keeping up appearances is important. But they can't keep their nice behaviour going for too long and when in a safe environment, they easily turn into a rude, arrogant and abusive person. It seems as if they have two different personalities. Again, their well-presented lovely persona to the outside world protects them from 'accusations' about their nasty traits, as other people simply don't believe they would behave badly.

My mother

She might start a huge argument before going out, having said the most terrible things, but she was able to just shake it off like a dog and step into a different behaviour. You wouldn't notice that anything had happened. What comes into play here as well is that she isn't emotionally affected in the way that most people are after an argument. Normal people want to talk it through, clear the air and get rid of the negative energy and emotions. However, she never felt the need to do so. It was an inconvenience at most.

The romantic partner

Narcissists want to confuse and by being loving, attentive and caring during a restaurant dinner (being seen by the world), they give the impression that all is well. Yet, before the front door has even opened, they might step into their vile behaviour and become manipulative, forceful and awful again.

Other examples

A sister met her narcissistic brother for lunch at his work and he was another person. Unrecognisable. Whereas at home he never listened to her and wasn't interested in her stories, now she seemed to have his full attention. Which was a weird experience.

The Narcissist Checklist

This is how my narcissist presents this trait:

....

....

....

....

How does this affect my happiness? (0-10) ....

How does this affect my stress levels? (0-10) ....

How strongly am I in control? (0-10) ....

How do I react to this situation/trait?

What do I feel?

....

....

....

What do I think?

....

....

....

How do I behave?

....

....

....

Notes

....

....

....

....

22. My narcissist will lie to suit their agenda

Narcissists will not let the truth get in the way of what they want. They make up stories, say you said things you never did and use information about others or situations to suit them.

My mother

Looking back, I can remember so many situations. She told me that the relationship between her and my sister was so close (golden child at that time) and that my sister had told her in confidence that she was raped when she was younger. What a great way to treat her confidence. To this day, I find it hard to believe and I think she just made it up.

She lied about money, pretending she had nothing, but my sister saw her current account when she helped her with her internet banking and it had a balance of 90,000 Euros.

She said my father had offered to buy her a Porsche, but she had declined the offer as it was too extravagant. Again, it wasn't true.

The romantic partner

Lying and twisting to create opportunities to control and make their partner feel bad is very common.

Accusations of infidelity make their partner run even harder for them in an attempt to prove that they didn't cheat. On the other hand, narcissists are known cheaters, as the admiration and confirmation of another person is a great way to get their Narcissistic Supply.

Other examples

Also, making up stories about being ill is also very common. To the extent, that they claim a cancer scare, a biopsy, heart attacks and other life-threatening illnesses.

The Narcissist Checklist

This is how my narcissist presents this trait:

How does this affect my happiness? (0-10) ....
How does this affect my stress levels? (0-10) ....
How strongly am I in control? (0-10) ....

How do I react to this situation/trait?

What do I feel?

What do I think?

How do I behave?

Notes

23. My narcissist reframes situations

Reframing is a technique where you change the perspective. Narcissists reframe situations to put other people down and leverage themselves.

My mother

When at high school, I was expected to make breakfast for my parents on a Saturday. This was to help relieve my dad, who made breakfast for my mother all week; he deserved some time off at the weekend. Instead of praising me, she would say how nice it was for me to be up and out early, so I had a longer day off to enjoy.

One year, I visited The Netherlands during an Easter weekend to visit my father in hospital. It ruined my family's Easter plans and we were all quite upset. When I left to return home my mother sneered that I had been lucky to get a break from my children.

The romantic partner

A woman's narcissistic husband didn't want her to go on holiday with her sister. However, as it was a long-standing tradition, he had to give in. She paid for it herself. When she got back, he had reframed the holiday as a present from him to her and positioned it as a gift.

Other examples

In a work situation, the manager always asks particular people to do extra work in their own time. Suggesting they might be eligible for a promotion. Yet when it comes to their performance review, he mentions they only worked extra because they were single and that a promotion was not to be expected.

This is how my narcissist presents this trait:

How does this affect my happiness? (0-10)
How does this affect my stress levels? (0-10)
How strongly am I in control? (0-10)

How do I react to this situation/trait?

What do I feel?

What do I think?

How do I behave?

Notes

24. My narcissist is good at gaslighting

Gaslighting is a tactic in which a person is manipulated to doubt their own reality and think they are going mad. It can manifest through continuous disagreement.

My mother

I know I paid for 90% of my university education. My parents always tell me that they paid, even though I can prove it with bank statements.

The romantic partner

Living together creates lots of opportunities for gaslighting. One lady knew that her passport was next to her bed as she needed it to go to a funeral of a friend abroad. When she woke up the passport had gone. She looked everywhere, couldn't find it in time and missed the occasion. Her narcissist told her she was so disorganised, that she hadn't put her passport next to her bed. 'Otherwise it would have been there.' Later, her partner came up and told her he found it in a cupboard, where, he said, she must have put it.

Her narcissist was at her all the time. Keeping an eye on everything she was doing; commenting, degrading, sneering, infantilising, laughing. It went on and on until she couldn't handle it anymore. She screamed and threw her phone at him. 'Stop it.' Afterwards, she felt awful about herself and her behaviour. He told her she was a psychopath. She was gaslighted.

Other examples

When a narcissist tells you something about yourself that you know is not true. But it then makes you reconsider. Like, you are always late. You start defending yourself, but at the same time, a bit of doubt creeps in.

The Narcissist Checklist

This is how my narcissist presents this trait:

How does this affect my happiness? (0-10)
How does this affect my stress levels? (0-10)
How strongly am I in control? (0-10)

How do I react to this situation/trait?

What do I feel?

What do I think?

How do I behave?

Notes

25. My narcissist is unreliable

Narcissists only consider themselves when it comes to arrangements. Is this the best for them? Is it the right time? The right activity? And earlier commitments can easily be dismissed in favour of a better option. How this affects other people doesn't come into the equation.

My mother

She would change the plans according to her mood. Told me to go clothes shopping with her that afternoon, only to cancel it last minute. Because there was a tennis arrangement.

She has never seen me or my sister play a hockey match. She would say she would come. She never did as there was something more interesting on offer.

The romantic partner

Evenings out are easily cancelled when work gets in the way or drinks with colleagues. For narcissists, it's never a big deal and they happily leave their partners in limbo until the last minute, only letting them know when it is already too late.

Other examples

Two friends had agreed on a day out to have a massive shopping spree for Christmas presents. When one of them asked, a few days before where they should meet and at what time, the narcissist said quite dismissively that she had signed up for a seminar that day and couldn't make it. She hadn't even bothered to tell her friend when she booked it.

This is how my narcissist presents this trait:

....

....

....

....

How does this affect my happiness? (0-10) ....

How does this affect my stress levels? (0-10) ....

How strongly am I in control? (0-10) ....

How do I react to this situation/trait?

What do I feel?

....

....

....

What do I think?

....

....

....

How do I behave?

....

....

....

Notes

....

....

....

....

26. My narcissist divides and rules

This is an effective strategy to cause havoc and unease in people around you. Through gossiping, lying and making up stories, it is easy to create a distance and unease between people. Another element of divide and rule is triangulation: the situation where a third person is being talked about or being seen as the 'messenger', always adding to confusion and doubt regarding others.

My mother

During a Christmas dinner in a restaurant, I danced with my uncle, who was married to my lovely aunt. He was a lovely man and we were very close. My mother sneered afterwards, suggesting there was a sexual attraction between us, aiming to upset my aunt, who I was also close to.

My sister and I discovered, unfortunately quite late in life, how she had been lying about situations and creating distrust between the two of us. She would say to me that my sister was really upset about my behaviour and therefore didn't want to see me. She told my sister that I looked down on her and thought it beneath me to be in touch.

The romantic partner

One narcissist mentioned to his partner how his mother didn't like her, but that he would stick with her. This created unease between all parties and prevented the natural development of a relationship between the mother in law and the partner.

Other examples

Gossip is a great platform for divide and rule. 'He said this about you' or 'I heard she is…' Or 'He asked me to let you know he can't make it as he is too busy'.

The Narcissist Checklist

This is how my narcissist presents this trait:

....
....
....

How does this affect my happiness? (0-10) ....
How does this affect my stress levels? (0-10) ....
How strongly am I in control? (0-10) ....

How do I react to this situation/trait?

What do I feel?

....
....
....

What do I think?

....
....
....

How do I behave?

....
....
....

Notes

....
....
....
....

27. My narcissist alienates family members and friends

This is particularly common within romantic relationships. It is very painful for parents to see their children getting involved with a narcissist. Not only are they unhappy, but they lose their confidence and ultimately, they lose themselves. A close relationship with family members is a threat to the narcissist, as this can help to undermine their power. Often this situation eats away at the victim as they feel torn between their partner and their family.

My mother

She would never encourage friendships. If anything, she would try to prevent them through being critical and dismissive about friends, pointing out their failures and always stressing how only one's family can be trusted.

The romantic partner

Narcissists will criticise a partner's family members, the relationships they have with them, their dependency, and will challenge situations as unhealthy. One woman spent the night with her family before going on a trip, as her family home was close to the airport. Her narcissist didn't want her to be with her family, offered a lift and then told her it was bad to depend on your family.

One woman missed Christmas dinner with her family because her narcissist booked a restaurant for just the two of them as a surprise. He didn't consult his partner, knowing she would have preferred spending Christmas with her family, instead of just with him.

Other examples

The friend who continuously criticises other friends you really love. This will eventually rub off and might make you doubt those friends.

This is how my narcissist presents this trait:

How does this affect my happiness? (0-10)
How does this affect my stress levels? (0-10)
How strongly am I in control? (0-10)

How do I react to this situation/trait?

What do I feel?

What do I think?

How do I behave?

Notes

28. My narcissist uses money and presents as a power tool

Money is power. So are presents. They can be used to bribe, to prompt action and be dangled like a golden carrot.

My mother

I paid for my university education and had a part-time job to fund it. As I didn't earn enough, I asked my parents for a loan. Which they gave me. However, I couldn't go on holiday or have any luxuries as that would prompt them to stop the loan. The moment I graduated they told me they wanted me to pay it back with a very high monthly payment. This would mean that I couldn't have a car, which I needed for work, didn't have money for weekends away or any other luxury. I went to a bank, got a loan and paid all the money back to them in one go. They never acknowledged it, never asked how I did it. It made me financially free from them, which was a great feeling. I guess they were seething with anger because of the loss of control.

The romantic partner

A narcissist might ask you to not work or work less, as they have enough money for the two of you. It makes you financially dependent on them and gives them power over you.

One woman who was setting up her own business would get frustrated and her narcissistic husband would say, 'Darling, just give it up.' Not out of love, but because it would give him more control.

Other examples

How about presents? People who buy you expensive presents might do so because they want to give you a treat. Narcissists buy presents because they want to impress others and get their Narcissistic Supply. Or they want to 'buy' you, so you do things for them and they can control your behaviour.

This is how my narcissist presents this trait:

How does this affect my happiness? (0-10)
How does this affect my stress levels? (0-10)
How strongly am I in control? (0-10)

How do I react to this situation/trait?

What do I feel?

What do I think?

How do I behave?

Notes

29. My narcissist parent chooses roles: golden child, scapegoat and the invisible one

In the family of a narcissist, the children get a role. These roles can change over time and are interchangeable. The three main roles are: 1) the golden child, who is supported, admired and feels loved, 2) the scapegoat, who is the black sheep and always gets the blame, 3) the invisible child, who is overlooked and ignored.

My mother

We had three children in our family. The eldest, the one who didn't fit in because of his disability, was the invisible one. As a result, he suffered quite a few unnecessary injuries – excessive sunburn, a head wound caused by glasses that were too tight, ingrown toenails. He was neglected, didn't exist.

I started off as the golden child but became the scapegoat. My sister started as the scapegoat and sort of ended up as the golden child. However, our roles switched regularly. All were aimed at preventing us from forming a strong bond and maybe turning against my mother.

It is very confusing to have different roles within a family and it evokes questions such as: Who am I? What am I? What is expected of me?

It feeds insecurity and lack of confidence as adults.

This is how my narcissist presents this trait:

....

....

....

....

How does this affect my happiness? (0-10) ....

How does this affect my stress levels? (0-10) ....

How strongly am I in control? (0-10) ....

How do I react to this situation/trait?

What do I feel?

....

....

....

What do I think?

....

....

....

How do I behave?

....

....

....

Notes

....

....

....

....

30. My narcissist is secretive about their finances

Money is power but if you know a their financial position they will lose their advantage in the game – the game where they can pretend to have no money or a lot of it. They are reluctant to be open.

My mother

My parents always pretended that money wasn't a problem and I think they threw it around for themselves quite happily (ski holidays, beautiful designer clothes, a car whenever they needed one). However, later in life, when they didn't seem to have any costs, and both received substantial incomes topped up with state pensions, I couldn't understand why they were moaning about lack of money.

The romantic partner

I have heard so many stories of people who have been cheated on by their narcissistic partner. Narcissists lie about costs, income and savings. They can do and pay for whatever they want, but there is never enough to do what their partner wants…

When it comes to a break-up or divorce, narcissists usually have a stack of money hidden in the background, which will help them to take control and pay high legal costs. One situation showed how the narcissist had emptied the joint savings account to pay his lawyer.

Other examples

We all know people who take advantage of whoever wants to pay – and it's never them. Narcissists moan about their financial situation and then all of a sudden are off on a luxury holiday in the Caribbean.

The Narcissist Checklist

This is how my narcissist presents this trait:

How does this affect my happiness? (0-10)
How does this affect my stress levels? (0-10)
How strongly am I in control? (0-10)

How do I react to this situation/trait?

What do I feel?

What do I think?

How do I behave?

Notes

31. My narcissist is good at emotional blackmail

Emotional blackmail taps into people's weaknesses, secrets or uses feelings of fear, obligation and guilt to make someone act and do as the blackmailer wishes.

My mother

When I became a student and lived in student accommodation, I came home each weekend to spend time with my brother. I had to, according to my parents, because I had the brains to go to university and have a great time during the week, but he would never be able to. Therefore, it was only fair that I came home and let him have fun, which got them 'off the hook'.

The romantic partner

Narcissists often tell their partner that they gave up so much for them, that it is only normal that their partner should give up things for them.

Other examples

You ask someone a favour and they remind you time and again as a way to make you do things for them.

> What do you mean 'I am abusive'?
> You are the abuser
> I have earned 8x more than you did,
> We went on holiday to amazing places
> I paid for that
> I paid most of the mortgage
> I paid and paid and paid
> You just looked after the kids
> As usual, you are mixing things up
> You are a parasite and a gold digger.
>
> Dr Mariette Jansen

This is how my narcissist presents this trait:

How does this affect my happiness? (0-10)
How does this affect my stress levels? (0-10)
How strongly am I in control? (0-10)

How do I react to this situation/trait?

What do I feel?

What do I think?

How do I behave?

Notes

32. My narcissist plays the victim

One way of getting attention is through playing the 'poor me' card. Narcissists often create drama with them as the victim. There is a psychological model, called the drama triangle (Stephen Karpman): victim, rescuer and prosecutor. The victim is powerless, can't help what is happening to them and needs to be rescued by someone. The victim doesn't take ownership of a situation or take responsibility. However, when the rescuer doesn't do exactly as they want, they turn from victim into prosecutor and target their attack towards the rescuer, turning them into the victim.

My mother

Our relationship has never been good. I have tried to explain in many ways what I thought didn't work or what we could change and she would still say: 'I don't know what I have done wrong. If you can't explain it properly, I clearly haven't done anything wrong. It is just in your mind; you just make it up. How can I change if you can't tell me what I have done wrong? This situation is caused by you, not by me. And look what you put me through.' This is infuriating.

I hadn't been in contact for years, but after my father died, I called my mother. In retrospect, this was a mistake because she took it as an invitation and a chance to be in contact again. She took to the habit of leaving me a short voicemail twice a week. 'Yeaaahhhh, it's mama. Can you call me back please?' Her voice trembled, she sounded emotional. Very dramatic, but she didn't give anything away. Did she want to talk about something specific? I translated her message as the familiar one 'You shall do as I say', just in a different format. The new voice, but still with the message 'Call me'. Very irritating and sometimes I was tempted to call and tell her to stop the phone calls, but that was exactly what she was hoping for. I am pleased I never did it.

The romantic partner

After or during an argument, when they get angry with you, narcissists will tell you that 'if only you had behaved differently, I wouldn't have had to lash out like that'. Again, they are the victim, they can't help it.

Other examples

The typical situation when someone blames others for their situation. Being late because the bus was delayed, being ill because they had to wait outside for the bus, being hungry because no one brought them food, being grumpy because their snoring partner kept them awake.

'What have I done to deserve this?
As my daughter I expect you to at least offer
Some help
Some attention,
Some money'
Which translates as:
'I have never done anything to deserve anything.
But as I am very special, I am entitled to
A lot of your help
All of your attention
All of your money
And anything else I can suck out of you,'

Dr Mariette Jansen

The Narcissist Checklist

This is how my narcissist presents this trait:

How does this affect my happiness? (0-10)
How does this affect my stress levels? (0-10)
How strongly am I in control? (0-10)

How do I react to this situation/trait?

What do I feel?

What do I think?

How do I behave?

Notes

33. My narcissist is exploitative

Exploitation is when you make use of or abuse other people for your own benefit.

My mother

In his later life, my brother was exploited to do the tasks and jobs around our parents' house. He wasn't well as his heart condition made him extremely tired, but he was sent on his bike to a shop far away for the best bread in town or summoned to pop over immediately if my parents wanted something.

The romantic partner

Financial exploitation is well-known in the life of the narcissist. Especially when the relationship is in its final stage and divorce or separation is being discussed. In earlier stages, there are often financial arrangements that are unfair and benefit the narcissist.

A narcissistic partner has no qualms about financially exploiting their partner.

Other examples

By playing the victim card – poor me, how can you solve this problem for me? – the narcissist can get others to go out of their way to help them out. This is how they start building their army of flying monkeys (Checklist point 10).

This is how my narcissist presents this trait:

How does this affect my happiness? (0-10)
How does this affect my stress levels? (0-10)
How strongly am I in control? (0-10)

How do I react to this situation/trait?

What do I feel?

What do I think?

How do I behave?

Notes

34. Very skilful at masking their narcissism

Often, they have developed some artificial skills that make other people think highly of them. They always seem to be interested in new people (to collect information they can use against them at a later stage), and they take actions that make them look good.

My mother

She would tell everyone how she always did everything for her children – cringe, cringe. How she supported my father, how she had chosen not to work as they didn't need the money and she would have taken an opportunity away from somebody else. Isn't that thoughtful?

When I decided to break contact with my parents, she played the role of the doting mother who didn't understand. She was devastated, a broken woman; she lost a lot of weight and got a lot of attention from people who felt sorry for her and then started bothering me (flying monkeys).

The romantic partner

Lots of narcissists are very generous in public. They are charming, buy drinks and come across very positively. Often, they seem the 'life and soul' of a party. It makes it difficult for the partner to 'moan' about someone who is so much fun. Often friends don't believe the negative sides of a narcissist and it feels very lonely.

Other examples

Someone who seems very chilled but is explosive in private situations. I picked up signals from a network acquaintance, who seemed to have unexpected, unpleasant and sudden fall-outs. I wondered what was going on as she came across nice enough. Until I was the target of a fall-out and saw her nasty side.

The Narcissist Checklist

This is how my narcissist presents this trait:

....

....

....

....

How does this affect my happiness? (0-10) ....
How does this affect my stress levels? (0-10) ....
How strongly am I in control? (0-10) ....

How do I react to this situation/trait?

What do I feel?

....

....

....

What do I think?

....

....

....

How do I behave?

....

....

....

Notes

....

....

....

....

5. CATEGORY IV:
Can't handle any form of criticism

Any form of negative feedback infuriates the narcissist and sparks nasty behaviour. This makes it impossible to discuss situations and events in an honest and open manner, as it is always the fault of others and never theirs. It is also the reason that there is limited scientific research on NPD as a narcissist is convinced that if someone is wrong, it is never them and they don't apply introspection or self-examination.

A narcissist's underlying insecurity is responsible for this. Their ego is fragile, and they usually have a strong negative attachment issue. They are convinced nobody can be trusted. To keep themselves safe, they won't let their vulnerability show and they work constantly to hide their real self.

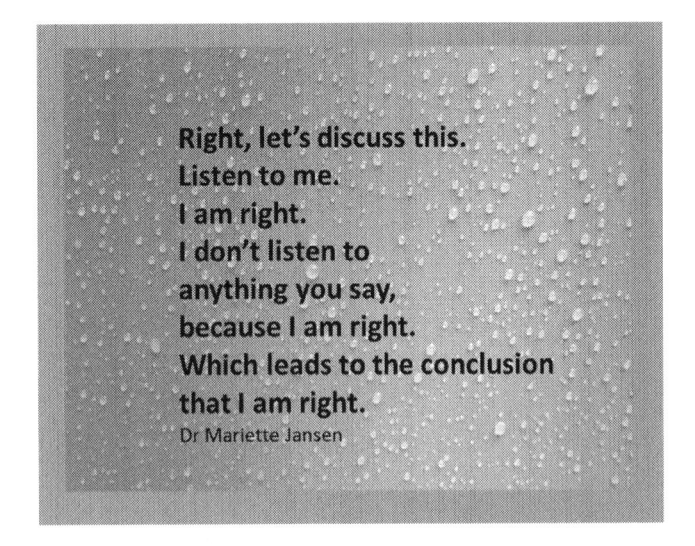

> Right, let's discuss this.
> Listen to me.
> I am right.
> I don't listen to anything you say, because I am right.
> Which leads to the conclusion that I am right.
> Dr Mariette Jansen

35. My narcissist can't handle any form of criticism

Any remark that could potentially be perceived as critical is picked up by the narcissist as a criticism. It means that people around them have to be very careful how they phrase what they want to say because a narcissist's reaction can be very aggressive and out of proportion – in comparison to normal people. However, narcissists see criticism as intensely humiliating as it threatens their vulnerable, fragile ego. It is not unusual for criticism to spark a 'Narcissistic Rage', which is extremely aggressive behaviour, sometimes violent and terrifying.

If you fancy a big argument, criticise a narcissist and you will know you have done something that is inappropriate in their eyes.

My mother

I can't really remember criticising her – I guess I didn't dare – apart from when I tried to explain how her behaviour affected me. This wasn't meant as a criticism, but as a way of exploring our relationship. We never had a proper discussion about this topic, which I now understand is due to the fact that she saw it as a criticism. She still asks, after 40 years, if I can explain properly what she has done wrong, because she doesn't understand and I am clearly not capable of explaining it to her.

The romantic partner

Narcissists continuously criticise their partners, but their partners are not allowed to do the same. Any criticism is cleverly turned against the partner and they are made to feel responsible or dismissed as being ridiculous, idiotic, psychotic, hysterical, bi-polar…

The narcissist's reaction to criticism is punishment, which can take the form of a cold shoulder, silent treatment, cancelling of outings.

Other examples

Often narcissists aim to persuade others to accept their point of view. Criticisms are not taken on board and it turns into a battle to get you on the same wavelength. It is their way of proving that you are wrong and they are right.

One guy decided to use snake poison as a supplement to prevent him from getting cancer. He was continuously trying to get people to do the same, desperately looking for approval and commenting on those who didn't as they 'too stupid to understand the value of natural remedies'.

This is how my narcissist presents this trait:

....

....

....

....

How does this affect my happiness? (0-10) ....

How does this affect my stress levels? (0-10) ....

How strongly am I in control? (0-10) ....

How do I react to this situation/trait?

What do I feel?

....

....

....

What do I think?

....

....

....

How do I behave?

....

....

....

Notes

....

....

....

....

36. My narcissist doesn't take ownership or responsibility when things go wrong

They are perfect and of course, don't make mistakes. They will not own the role they play when things go wrong. They believe they are the victims of other people's actions and decisions and they don't hesitate to point the blame elsewhere.

There might be situations when squeesing out a false apology can't be avoided, a fauxpology, which is meant to deflect or induce guilt. Along the lines of 'I'm sorry that you are so sensitive' or 'Sorry that you are too stupid to understand'.

My mother

When I lived in the student house, which my parents had bought, I was made responsible for collecting the rent. The first time I reported that the girl in the room next to me hadn't paid, my mother said: 'Well, you chose here to live there.'

The romantic partner

Whatever goes wrong, like a holiday booking, the weather on holiday or the 'fun' during a holiday – anything that doesn't work – the partner is blamed. Even if it is nothing that you could blame anyone for.

The partner will be blamed for the behaviour of the narcissist.

Other examples

The boss who manages to find the person in his team, or in someone else's team, who screwed it all up… The one who has to take the blame.

The Narcissist Checklist

This is how my narcissist presents this trait:

How does this affect my happiness? (0-10)
How does this affect my stress levels? (0-10)
How strongly am I in control? (0-10)

How do I react to this situation/trait?

What do I feel?

What do I think?

How do I behave?

Notes

37. My narcissist gets angry about contrary viewpoints

They can't be challenged about their viewpoints, as this might reveal them as not the perfect person they need to be seen as. Healthy people discuss viewpoints and allow each person to have theirs. For a narcissist, it is a sign of betrayal. 'How dare you think differently? I know best.'

My mother

When I was about 10, we discussed social equality and human rights, and I was passionate about giving everyone the same chances and opportunities. Very left-wing. My mother spat at me with furious eyes and called me 'rooie rat', a very dismissive Dutch saying for a socialist.

The romantic partner

Narcissists love debates, as long as they come out at the winning end. If not, peace is not to be found. Most partners, therefore, agree with them, for the sake of peace.

Other examples

Narcissists are the type of people who at a party will nail you down and keep on talking to you about whatever it is they want to talk about. They are annoying, as it is hard to get away from them.

They will also be critical of politicians and get very angry and agitated, because they know better than all those 'tossers' who make decisions.

The Narcissist Checklist

This is how my narcissist presents this trait:

How does this affect my happiness? (0-10)
How does this affect my stress levels? (0-10)
How strongly am I in control? (0-10)

How do I react to this situation/trait?

What do I feel?

What do I think?

How do I behave?

Notes

38. My narcissist is keen to point out what is wrong in others

With their external focus, narcissists continuously judge others and point out, rightly or wrongly, what they do wrong.

My mother

My mother was a master at telling me what was not good about me and also loved talking about others and what they did wrong. I discovered later that a lot of this didn't represent the truth but was based on her fantasy.

Doctors, estate agents, solicitors, surveyors always makes mistakes and she will find those.

The romantic partner

This is one of the reasons that the partner of a narcissist will lose self-esteem and confidence, as everything they do will often be marked as wrong. You cooked potatoes but should have baked them. You leave early but should have offered a lift. You bought a skirt, but it should have been a dress. Any action may be criticised and marked as 'wrong'.

Other examples

In the friendship sphere, it is great material for gossip. A narcissist will happily talk about other people's shortcomings.

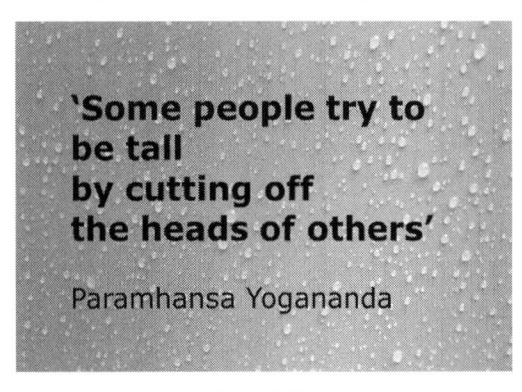

> 'Some people try to be tall by cutting off the heads of others'
>
> Paramhansa Yogananda

This is how my narcissist presents this trait:

....
....
....
....

How does this affect my happiness? (0-10) ....
How does this affect my stress levels? (0-10) ....
How strongly am I in control? (0-10) ....

How do I react to this situation/trait?

What do I feel?

....
....
....

What do I think?

....
....
....

How do I behave?

....
....
....

Notes

....
....
....
....

39. My narcissist never makes mistakes

Narcissists believe they are perfect. Mistakes are made by others, not by them. If you point out that they have made a mistake, they will never own up to it but blame the situation or other people, and will make up a story that means they are not responsible for what happened. And they will look to punish you for embarrassing them.

My mother

Saying to her 'You did that wrong' created a tense situation and a response along the lines of 'How dare you say that to me?' or my father would interfere and tell me off.

The romantic partner

If a narcissist's partner points out a mistake, it will be war. Partners consequently cover up their own mistakes and don't mention them. They also make excuses for the mistakes of the narcissist.

Other examples

People at work who are always right. In a meeting, they are the 'I know it all' attendees.

This is how my narcissist presents this trait:

....

....

....

....

....

How does this affect my happiness? (0-10) ....

How does this affect my stress levels? (0-10) ....

How strongly am I in control? (0-10) ....

How do I react to this situation/trait?

What do I feel?

....

....

....

What do I think?

....

....

....

How do I behave?

....

....

....

Notes

....

....

....

....

40. My narcissist considers every situation in the light of winning

Life is not about being but about going for the win. Narcissists are excellent salespeople as they never give up and go for 'the kill'. They don't accept no as this is seen as a personal attack and they will carry on working on the task. Until they have won.

My mother

After my father died, I called her, once. As the call presented the same situation as always (me being told off about how wrong I am and what a terrible person I am and her complaining about her life and asking for attention), it was clear to me that I made the right decision a few years earlier to cut the cords. After this phone call, she expected me to be available for contact again and for about four months twice a week she would leave a voicemail, summoning me to call her. She didn't really want me, as a person, but she wanted to win this situation.

The romantic partner

Anyone who has been with a narcissist will have experienced endless situations where the discussions could only end after the acknowledgement that they were right. Regardless of the subject of the discussion. They needed to hear that they were right. Many partners give in for the sake of peace.

Other examples

Lots of narcissists are very successful in business situations. This is due to the need to win, combined with a lack of empathy. Ruthless politicians, entrepreneurs and leaders have a lot of narcissistic traits. Think how Donald Trump dealt with Covid-19: he manipulated the facts and keen to come out as the 'winner'.

This is how my narcissist presents this trait:

How does this affect my happiness? (0-10)
How does this affect my stress levels? (0-10)
How strongly am I in control? (0-10)

How do I react to this situation/trait?

What do I feel?

What do I think?

How do I behave?

Notes

6. CATEGORY V:
Lacks empathy and emotional awareness

Narcissists are cut off from their emotions. The only emotions they know are fear, envy, hate and anger. They don't understand the emotional world of others and are not interested either. They can't comprehend upset. They are quick to throw remarks about people who are in touch with their emotions as hysterical, psychotic and other inappropriate words. They simply don't get it. It makes them feel uncomfortable, because how can you control something you don't understand? Emotions are a threat to the need for security. Their lack of empathy makes it easy for them to be manipulative, exploitative and cruel. With a total lack of emotional awareness, their natural state is being cold and distant.

Brain scans of people with Narcissistic Personality Disorder (NPD) showed they have less brain matter in areas associated with emotional empathy. This suggests that the lack of empathy is due to a physical difference and may explain why narcissists don't change.

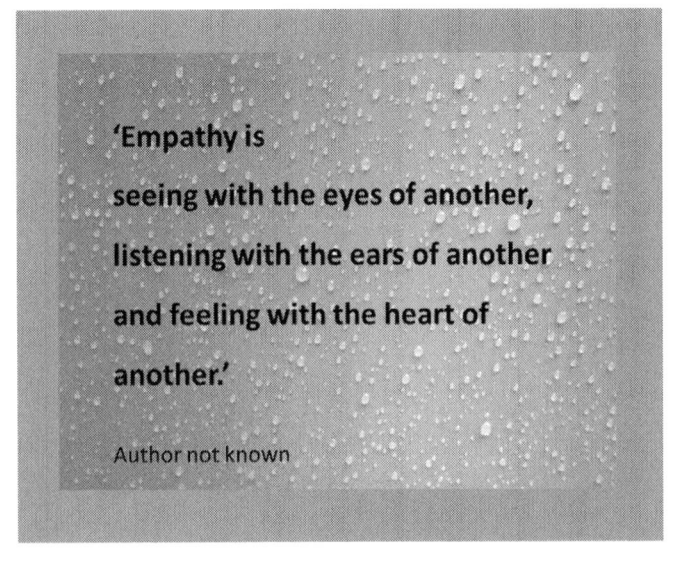

> 'Empathy is seeing with the eyes of another, listening with the ears of another and feeling with the heart of another.'
>
> Author not known

41. My narcissist lacks empathy

Narcissists have a total lack of imagination on how other people might feel or think. They are not open to hearing about it and they lack consideration for others. This is one of the most significant indicators of a narcissist: a total lack of empathy. Their lack of empathy also makes them cruel and insensitive in their actions and their words.

My mother

She couldn't care less about other people's wishes or circumstances. She only considers what she wants. When I was eight, I had tonsillitis and went into hospital for a small operation. Coming home, I had to go straight into my bedroom and stay there. Because, when you are sick, you stay in bed. And your bed is in the bedroom. My father came to check on me later that day, gave me some water and left. It was a long, long day. The next day I developed a fever and felt miserable and hot. That was the only moment I remember my mother putting her cool hand on my forehead and that was incredibly comforting and surprising.

The romantic partner

Whether you need to feel supported in a challenge, whether you crave some attention, or whether you simply want to feel understood, you won't get it from your narcissistic partner. Narcissists will remain cold and at a distance and you will feel alone and lonely. A terrible example was given by a lady who had just miscarried. Her husband kept on buying baby clothes, 'So you are ready for the next one.'

Other examples

When a woman shared that her holiday had been cancelled due to an issue with her passport, her narcissist friend shrugged her shoulders and started to talk about her own upcoming holiday. How insensitive is that?

The phrase: 'That must be so hard for you' doesn't exist in a narcissist's vocabulary.

> **Empathy is connected with loving, giving and caring. If you don't know what it means to love, give and care, you won't be able to understand empathy. Ever.**
> Dr Mariette Jansen

This is how my narcissist presents this trait:

How does this affect my happiness? (0-10)
How does this affect my stress levels? (0-10)
How strongly am I in control? (0-10)

How do I react to this situation/trait?

What do I feel?

What do I think?

How do I behave?

Notes

42. My narcissist laughs at other's misfortune – Schadenfreude

It's a narcissist's wet dream to hear about people's pain and misfortune. They thrive on hearing those stories. Even better, when they can see it for themselves. When sharing, they will enter into lots of details and elaborate forever.

My mother

My sister was a coeliac and when she had unintentionally eaten something she couldn't stomach, she would be violently ill and needed a recovery time of a few days. My mother hardly ever called me but she loved to get in touch and tell me all about my sister's situation, and I could hear the smile in her voice. She absolutely enjoyed it.

The romantic partner

This is where cruelty and physical abuse comes in. How about the narcissist, who locked his partner out in the dark and the cold. And then later on reminded them how cold and wet they had become and how awful they looked. Smirking and laughing when telling the story to others.

Other examples

Narcissists love to talk about people's illnesses and conditions. Even when they overstep boundaries of private information, they don't care.

This is how my narcissist presents this trait:

How does this affect my happiness? (0-10)
How does this affect my stress levels? (0-10)
How strongly am I in control? (0-10)

How do I react to this situation/trait?

What do I feel?

What do I think?

How do I behave?

Notes

43. My narcissist takes everything literally

Narcissists don't have free-flowing minds. They lack creative thinking as that would take them into the world of fantasy and creativity. They can't go there as they are on the lookout for danger all the time. Fantasy and imagination is confusing to them. Literal language gives clarity and safety; metaphors, playful language and jokes carry an element of danger.

My mother

When in a conversation and a poetic description comes up, she doesn't get it and feels clearly uncomfortable. She always has to bring it back to 'So this means xx or yy'.

The romantic partner

Narcissists are very unimaginative. Poetic language, romantic words are all taken literally. A loving 'you look like a puppy' doesn't go down well because they would find the literal meaning not flattering enough and possibly insulting.

Other examples

Any metaphor is lost, any joke becomes the 'wrong thing' to have said.

This is how my narcissist presents this trait:

....

....

....

....

How does this affect my happiness? (0-10) ....

How does this affect my stress levels? (0-10) ....

How strongly am I in control? (0-10) ....

How do I react to this situation/trait?

What do I feel?

....

....

....

What do I think?

....

....

....

How do I behave?

....

....

....

Notes

....

....

....

....

....

44. My narcissist thinks in black and white

Similar to why narcissists take language literally (to understand and feel safe), they hold onto black and white thinking. Wrong or right. Danger or safety. There is no space for grey areas because that makes them feel insecure. Once they have made up their minds, it is black or white. No movement is possible.

My mother

Once you've said something, that's it. It will be true forever. She thinks the same as when she was 25. That concept was applied to us children as well. If you liked strawberry ice cream when you were 8, it should stay your favourite ice cream for the rest of your life. If she remembered, that is.

The romantic partner

Anyone in a relationship with a narcissist will know how a situation is either good or bad. How you are a great partner or a disaster. There is no middle ground.

Other examples

Anyone who is insecure hangs onto a firm opinion to mask their insecurity. And you will not be able to have an engaging conversation.

This is how my narcissist presents this trait:

How does this affect my happiness? (0-10)
How does this affect my stress levels? (0-10)
How strongly am I in control? (0-10)

How do I react to this situation/trait?

What do I feel?

What do I think?

How do I behave?

Notes

45. My narcissist is suspicious

A Dutch proverb says it very clearly: 'The innkeeper trusts his guests after his own character'. Narcissists are suspicious of traits that they have themselves. They do not trust other's words and actions. They know how easy it is to talk and act with negative intentions.

My mother

My parents were always telling us that there were lots of people around who would take financial advantage of vulnerable people like my brother. And yet, the only situation I know of where he was taken advantage of was…by my parents.

The romantic partner

It is well-known that narcissists are always on the lookout for adultery, committed by their partner. Just talking to someone, coming home late, sending a private text are all signals to kick off the accusation that you are looking at other people, flirting or even being unfaithful. But they are known themselves for being cheating and unfaithful.

Other examples

In connection with anyone, notice what is being said about others. Could it be that it is applicable to them?

This is how my narcissist presents this trait:

_____
_____
_____
_____

How does this affect my happiness? (0-10) _____
How does this affect my stress levels? (0-10) _____
How strongly am I in control? (0-10) _____

How do I react to this situation/trait?

What do I feel?

_____
_____
_____

What do I think?

_____
_____
_____

How do I behave?

_____
_____
_____

Notes

_____
_____
_____
_____

46. My narcissist can be very cruel

Their lack of empathy and emotional awareness means that narcissists look at situations very differently from 'normal' people. They look at situations practically and pragmatically and bypass unkindness and cruelty with a shrug of the shoulder. They just don't get it.

My mother

Especially towards my brother, she could be very mean. One day he was due to visit me at my student house to celebrate my birthday. This was during a time that I didn't want contact with my parents. He was very excited, and my mother had promised to bake an apple loaf he could bring to me. Then she used it as a tool to make him do things: 'Otherwise I am not baking the loaf'. It also made him extra nervous to come over.

Another time she chose to not notice that his glasses were too tight until he was bleeding behind his ears and had developed ulcers.

The romantic partner

Another situation was where a couple lived in a house with one toilet. The narcissist made it a habit of quickly jumping into the bathroom just before his partner wanted to get in and then locked the door for a long time. The partner was sometimes forced out of the house to go to the toilet at the neighbours.

One narcissistic husband saw his wife fall down the stairs. He left her in agony and went out to get his car cleaned and get fuel. After an hour, he returned and only then called an ambulance.

Other examples

The man who drove his car on a country road, noticed a pheasant crossing the road, accelerated and ran it over. He smiled and said: 'Stupid beast, should have looked before crossing'.

The Narcissist Checklist

This is how my narcissist presents this trait:

....

....

....

....

How does this affect my happiness? (0-10) ....

How does this affect my stress levels? (0-10) ....

How strongly am I in control? (0-10) ....

How do I react to this situation/trait?

What do I feel?

....

....

....

What do I think?

....

....

....

How do I behave?

....

....

....

Notes

....

....

....

....

47. My narcissist can't discuss emotional issues

Emotions are unknown territory for narcissists. As a result, they can't talk about them. Emotions and emotional people make them uncomfortable and they will do anything to move away from them.

My mother

I have cried, shouted, tried to communicate how I felt. No success. Had I understood what was going on in her head, I would have stopped trying to make her understand much earlier. She called me hysterical when I showed emotions and it never brought us any closer.

The romantic partner

Narcissists quickly move away from emotions and switch to practical and pragmatic conversations instead. Or they may use an emotional outburst as a way to gaslight and manipulate. 'You always seem to be critical of me, but you can't tell me what I have done wrong. It's just your imagination.'

When the relationship is revolving around practical actions, it can work. The moment the projects are finished it will be harder to find meaning in the cooperation as emotions are not there.

Other examples

When a narcissist visited her friend, who had just been diagnosed with cancer, they didn't talk about the illness or anything related to it. It felt like the narcissist did the 'right' thing for the benefit of the outside world, which is visiting, but she didn't offer any emotional support.

This is how my narcissist presents this trait:

How does this affect my happiness? (0-10)
How does this affect my stress levels? (0-10)
How strongly am I in control? (0-10)

How do I react to this situation/trait?

What do I feel?

What do I think?

How do I behave?

Notes

48. My narcissist is not interested in other people

An indicator that reveals a narcissist is their behaviour in a group. When someone else is the centre of attention they will try to change that by interrupting. Or they will look away with that 'I am really bored' look. They usually don't remember what others have told them unless they can use it for ammunition later.

My mother

Numerous times she asked me what I actually did for a living and what my husband's job was… but she never remembered.

She could pretend to show an interest but often asked inappropriate questions. She couldn't remember what my husband did for a living, but she wanted to know how much he earned.

The romantic partner

The interest a narcissistic partner has in you is that your function is to offer the Narcissistic Supply. Other people are only of interest if they can do the same or support the status of the narcissist.

Other examples

Small talk during a reception is a great observation area. People who are interested in people will engage, even if the topic of conversation is shallow. Narcissists will check you out and move away quickly if there is nothing to be gained by talking to you.

This is how my narcissist presents this trait:

How does this affect my happiness? (0-10)
How does this affect my stress levels? (0-10)
How strongly am I in control? (0-10)

How do I react to this situation/trait?

What do I feel?

What do I think?

How do I behave?

Notes

49. My narcissist has no self-awareness

Narcissists are externally focussed. They are looking for their Narcissistic Supply, which has to come from other people. Their internal focus is nihil or non-existent. As they are convinced that they are perfect, there is no point in self-reflection. One of the challenges in the research of narcissism is that they won't admit themselves to therapy and as a result there is not a lot known about them.

Narcissists don't pick up on signals from others about their behaviour and they don't care.

My mother

She had no idea that she scared people, that my sister absolutely hated her or that people didn't find her sympathetic. My father called her sweet, loving, caring, wonderful and more, and that was enough confirmation.

The romantic partner

It is difficult to connect on a deeper level with a narcissist as the starting point is that they know it all and are not open to exploring what goes on in them which makes the relationship difficult. Often narcissists project their shortcomings onto their partner, but they don't know that they are actually talking about themselves (projection).

Other examples

Narcissists cannot talk about themselves in an emotional way. They don't recognise feelings. They don't know how to come to a decision. They don't contemplate a situation and their role in it. They only point the finger at others, never at themselves.

This is how my narcissist presents this trait:

How does this affect my happiness? (0-10)
How does this affect my stress levels? (0-10)
How strongly am I in control? (0-10)

How do I react to this situation/trait?

What do I feel?

What do I think?

How do I behave?

Notes

50. My narcissist is emotionally distant and unavailable

Narcissists have no emotions – apart from anger, envy, hate and fear. You can't connect with a lack of emotions and you can't share what is not there. You can't understand what you don't know and that is exactly where the narcissist is when it comes to emotions.

My mother

Whenever I wanted to talk about how I felt, she couldn't give a response. She would glance over at me, wriggle a bit and walk away or change the subject. It left me feeling cold and misunderstood.

The romantic partner

The relationship might be very focused on action focussed 'doing', such as organising your house or arranging a holiday. Actions and practicalities work well; feelings and emotions are a no-go area. Narcissists are unable to give emotional support in challenging times.

Other examples

A good checkpoint for gauging someone's level of narcissism is when you are looking for emotional support. Are they there for you, do they emotionally connect or are you left to your own devices? Do they help you with practicalities, but are not with you when you just want to share emotions?

This is how my narcissist presents this trait:

How does this affect my happiness? (0-10)
How does this affect my stress levels? (0-10)
How strongly am I in control? (0-10)

How do I react to this situation/trait?

What do I feel?

What do I think?

How do I behave?

Notes

Part IV: Frequently Asked Questions about Narcissism

Introduction

Once you know you have a narcissist in your life, you gain an instant understanding of certain situations. It also leaves a lot to be questioned. I have collected a number of questions in relation to narcissism and, if appropriate, added advice.

Questions and answers

Q: Why is a narcissist called a narcissist?

One of the tragic stories in Greek Mythology is the love story about Narcissus and Echo. Narcissus was a handsome hunter who broke the hearts of many. He was aloof, arrogant and dismissive of women. One day the forest nymph Echo fell in love with him but he humiliated and rejected her, saying 'May I die before you enjoy my body'. Echo wasted away, obsessed still with Narcissus and suffering from depression. Nemesis, the goddess of revenge, punished Narcissus for his cruel behaviour by making him fall in love with himself. When Narcissus saw his reflection in a pond, love overtook him. He believed that he'd finally found someone worthy of his love and became entirely absorbed with his own beautiful image. Suffering this unobtainable love, he eventually took his own life, leaving a flower in his place.

Q: What is the best way to find out if someone is a narcissist?

The easiest way to test this out is by disagreeing with them and criticising them. A narcissist's reaction will be very strong and out of proportion. They won't want to explore and discuss; they just want to be right. They won't stop until they receive confirmation that they are in the right or they will go off in a huff.

Q: My partner always wants attention. When she is in the pub, she literally buys attention by offering drinks to everyone. When it is just the two of us, she wants my full attention the whole time. It is tiring and I sometimes want to do my own thing. How can I change her?

First things first. You will not be able to change her. You can only change the way you respond to her attention-seeking. If you don't give her what she wants, what is the consequence? Does she punish you by ignoring you or putting you down?

She needs attention to feel important. If she doesn't get it, she will be angry and moody and take it out on you.

However, if you don't want to 'spoil' her with attention when you are together, I suggest you physically remove yourself from the scene. Do something elsewhere. That is the best way to avoid her direct or indirect requests.

Q: My boyfriend is always a bit dismissive of me. I have tried to end the relationship four times now, but every time I went back. He almost smirks, saying 'I knew it. I knew you would come back to me.' Why do I go back?

Maybe it is time for some contemplation and navel-gazing. What is it you get out of the relationship? What inspires you to go back each time? Could it be there is something inside you that wants to prove that you can actually make him more appreciative of you? Are you doing your best to make that happen? Do you want to rescue him? Do you think you can't live without him? Do you feel guilty? I wonder if you value yourself. Often people who don't think they are good enough, accept being treated with dismissiveness and disrespect. As if you don't deserve better... If that is the case, it is important to build a new relationship with yourself. If you value and love yourself, you wouldn't want to be in a relationship with someone who doesn't.

Q: When my friend and I go shopping, she always goes for the label, even if it doesn't look good. My budget is tight and often I don't want to buy her designer choice for me, but she gets really stroppy with me. Why?

It is important for your friend to be seen with people who support her vision of the world. She clearly likes her labels as they make her feel good. For her, the label, which represents status and prestige, is more important than how the actual garment looks on you. She wants to surround herself with people who appear to support her values and looks.

It's up to you if you want to accommodate her views and buy clothes that you don't like… or find a way to still go shopping, but not let her dictate what you need to buy. Maybe just tell her you already have a top in that colour or that you don't need trousers. And notice how she responds to that.

Q: I fell in love with this wonderful girl. But now we are further into the relationship, I am not sure if it is all wonderful. It is, as long as I do as she tells me. Most of the time I don't mind, but there have been a few situations when I've had to take a deep breath and push my ideas to the side. Do you think I am with a narcissist?

You might be and you might not. It is difficult to give a straight answer based on the information you've given. What is important is that you set boundaries. What is really you? What is really important to you? And for you to stick to that.

Nobody should have to give up stuff that is important to them just because they are in a relationship. You can give, you can take, but you shouldn't give up things that really matter to you. Be clear to yourself about those priorities. Don't give in when it comes to those and then see what happens.

Q: Whenever I share something personal and important, it is almost thrown back at me as not interesting or not as important as what he is doing. I don't know what to talk about without causing this insecurity in me.

You haven't mentioned who you are sharing with. Your partner? Then it doesn't sound like a balanced and healthy relationship. Should you continue to share? Your friend? This also sounds unbalanced. What is the friendship based on? Can you avoid sharing personal information and still continue the friendship? Your family? What are your reasons for sharing important and personal information if you know you won't receive respect and acknowledgement? . If you don't want to hear that they are doing better than you, maybe just leave it.

If you want to have conversations, you could think of impersonal topics that are of no interest to you but keep a dialogue going. My two main go-to topics in phone conversations with my parents were Wimbledon (I couldn't care less, but they could talk forever about a Wimbledon match or incident) or the weather. And, guess what? The weather was always sunnier, dryer and warmer where they were. It was a way for me to give them Narcissistic Supply without it taking away anything from me. What could be your safe topics?

Q: My boyfriend really wants to 'brag' about our holiday destinations and let everybody know we went to Davos, Capri and Hawaii. In St Tropez, we just had a plate with pasta and a water and paid 80 Euros. I can't afford it. I would prefer

to go camping in France, swim in the local river and have a BBQ at a campsite. What should I do?

It sounds as if you have already invested money into the dreams and wishes of your narcissistic partner. One way of not being lured into colluding with him and joining him on his expensive adventures is to keep your budget separate. It is not fair for you to fund his choices and find yourself in financial difficulty because of it.

Of course, your boyfriend might offer to give you some money towards the holiday, but that would also give him more power and control over you.

Q: I don't know what is going on with my girlfriend. She seems moody, but her moods are connected with the company she is in and where she is. When she is with me at home or with her family, she is foul and hostile. When we are out, she is fun and fabulous. I wonder what sparks her mood change and what I can do about it?

Your girlfriend is working hard to keep up appearances and showing other people her positive sides. However, this is tiring and when she feels safe, she can just be who she really is. Her mood has nothing to do with you, but everything to do with her. Are you prepared to live with someone whose realness is moody?

Q: When I compare my mother to the mothers of my friends, she is so different. She is less chatty than them, seems not at all interested and is quite boring. Still every day I have to tell her what a great mum she is. I am fed up with it because she isn't. How can I break that cycle?

It seems that in your family a few rules have been set. One of them is to offer your mother her Narcissistic Supply. She needs that and I wonder, what will happen if you deny her that? Your family members might turn against you. Think about whether that will help you. Is there a way you can recognise other traits and start to make small changes which will subtly show that you are not totally cooperating with the admiration pressure? Be gentle, don't throw the cat amongst the pigeons as this will not serve you. Take it one baby step at a time.

Q: When I was single, I helped my parents quite a lot. I took them shopping on a Saturday, took them to their activities and often picked them up. Now I am in a relationship, and I want to spend time with my girlfriend. However, my parents are still expecting the same 'service' from me. I tried to explain that I have less time now, but my mother was absolutely vile. She was verbally aggressive and hasn't spoken to me since. I feel absolutely terrible. My siblings all have families themselves and are very busy.

You have been very kind to your parents and generous with your time when you had the time. Now your situation has changed and so have your priorities. I understand it is difficult, especially for your mother, to not have you available like before. You have given her your time voluntarily and she doesn't have any rights to your time. You are entitled to your own time. However, often habits can turn into unreasonable expectations. That is not the way your mother looks at it and she will see this habit as something she is entitled to. Is there a way you can 'solve' her issue that lets you off the hook? Can someone else take over what you did for her? Even if you find a solution, she will still feel angry with you as you have decided to prioritise something or someone else over her. The best way is to be very clear about you not being available all the time and leave it at that. (JADE is the best communication technique – see Part VI).

Q: I have realised I don't want to go out with my partner to a restaurant. She always complains aggressively and sends her food back. Often, she refuses another dish, making remarks regarding the bad quality of the food. I know she is wrong as we go to reputable places and I enjoy my food. What should I do?

If the behaviour of your partner spoils your dinner, you are quite right to not go out with her anymore. It makes her feel important and powerful when she can put other people down, but you don't have to collude with her or offer her the opportunity by taking her nice to nice places.

Q: My mother doesn't want to queue. She is too important to have to wait her turn. When we go out somewhere she takes a walking stick so she can pretend she is physically unwell and should get priority. I feel ashamed to be with her because I know it is just an act. What can I do?

Do you go with her to the front of the queue? If so, you collude with her and facilitate her to abuse others. What would happen if you stayed in the queue and she had to wait for you anyway?

Q: How do I approach my friend, who never pays when we are out together? She forgets her wallet, loses her card or can't afford to pay. I always end up paying for her. When I ask for the money back, she sounds surprised and seems to have forgotten all about it. How can I deal with that better?

Even though you might miss out on outings with your friend, I think the best way forward is to keep your hand in your pocket next time you are out with her and make her pay. Or if she can't, let her feel the consequences and sort it out. It might show her in a new light and also dent the friendship, but that is the risk of a reality check.

Q: I have been in a relationship for two years now and even though we have a good time, I think something is missing. We do a lot of things; we exercise together, we just bought a house which we are doing up and we both have busy jobs. It seems

we are always focused on action and I am starting to miss moments of calm and intimacy. How can I bring that in?

If your partner is a narcissist, your relationship will not be emotionally intimate for the simple fact that they don't recognise emotions. If it is not there, that's it. Work out for yourself how you could 'test' your partner. Share emotional subjects and observe their response. If it is dismissive of your feelings and they move away from the topic towards practical issues, you have to accept that emotions are not part of your relationship. Then you have to decide if there is enough to keep going. Good luck.

Q: My boyfriend is very self-centred. He wants to be the centre of attention and always tells other people he is the best. It is annoying and boring. Does that make him a narcissist?

Narcissism is a sliding scale. The people I have interviewed about their narcissist scored 40 or more on my checklist. That is a clear indication. However, your boyfriend could have a few traits, which might mean he is 'on the spectrum' but not a full-blown narcissist. Go through the checklist with him in mind and see where he ends up.

> I aim to be the star of every show or every episode. I shine so brightly that I blind those around me, so they can't see me for who I really am.
>
> Dr Mariette Jansen

Q: I can't get my head around my partner. He seems to be like two different people: charming, loving and attentive, but then he changes and becomes rude, cynical and dismissive. It drives me crazy, as I love the positive him as much as I hate the negative him. Who is the real one?

Unfortunately, the real one is the negative one – the one who is unpleasant and feels better when bullying others or putting them down. It gives them a sense of control (safety), which they need as they are hiding their fragile ego. It also makes them feel better than you as they seem to control you and your feelings. The way to get a grip on this is to start writing down the numerous situations in detail and document events and your feelings.

Q: The narcissist in my life always gives me the cold shoulder when I try to explain how I feel. Does it mean I should give up trying?

It is important to remember that your emotional communication will not be received. If you know that, what is then the point of trying? It will give ammunition to the narcissist to manipulate you or talk about you to others in a bad way. Accept that emotions are not a useful topic of conversation.

Q: My friend's husband is critical and negative about me. He doesn't want her to see me so we always meet in secret. Also, I am not allowed to tell anyone I am seeing her. That feels really uncomfortable as I am an open and honest person.

Meeting your friend is important to you, but honouring your values of being open and honest is also important. This is the knock-on effect a narcissist can have on relationships. Your friend wants you to behave against your principles because of her husband. It is time to reconsider if the friendship is worth giving up your values for… Narcissistic relationships and friendships always carry elements of dishonesty. Do you want to be infected?

Part V:
Claim your victory

Introduction

Beating the narcissist requires two levels: you don't give them what they want (Narcissistic Supply) and you keep yourself safe, sane and happy.

The most effective way to do the latter is to run. Move away from your narcissist or remove them from your life.

However, as narcissists are very clever at masking their narcissism, it usually takes a while (sometimes decades) to discover who and what you are dealing with. By then, you are knee-deep in it and running away has complications.

If running away from a narcissistic parent, you will most likely lose a lot of family members in the process.

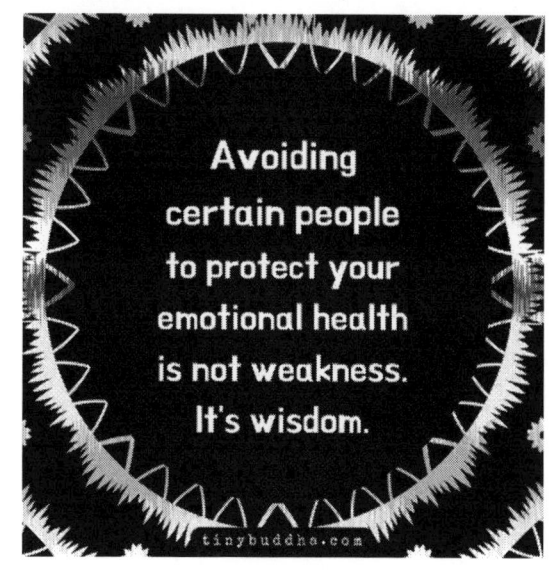

> Avoiding certain people to protect your emotional health is not weakness. It's wisdom.
>
> tinybuddha.com

When you are the victim of a narcissist, you will be made to feel powerless. Caged and completely unaware of how to get out of the cage. The victim mentality is all about the belief that you are helpless and it feels hopeless.

The victor is the person who knows they are in control of their life. And if they are not there yet, they know they are on their way and will get there. A victor welcomes the challenges of life, loves overcoming them and thrives.

The victor thinks and behaves very differently from a victim, and in this chapter, I will present you with the skills and tools to become the victor.

1. Confusion

There is never a winner in the relationship with a narcissist. Narcissists are always the loser as they will never obtain happiness, love and contentment. Unfortunately, they also destroy the chances for others on happiness, love and contentment. Which is pretty grim.

All the narcissist's actions are aimed at them feeling safe and satisfied. Feeling safe means that their true self, their fragile ego, is invisible. They need to be seen as strong and special and not as vulnerable and insecure.

The satisfaction comes from the Narcissistic Supply, the external feed of admiration, attention, confirmation and being in control. How do they secure their safety and satisfaction? Through creating confusion. Someone who is confused is not confident and easier to control. The focus of all their actions is on making others feel small and insignificant, because then the narcissist will be bigger, in control and 'safe'.

There is a range of very effective techniques narcissists use which work very well. Some of these can be difficult to spot. At first. They are presented very skilfully and instead of noticing the manipulation, victims often start to doubt themselves.

An indication that something is not right, would be how you feel around someone. When you feel regularly upset, misunderstood, can't really connect, feel put-down and are confused, you might be the victim of a narcissist's clever manipulation techniques.

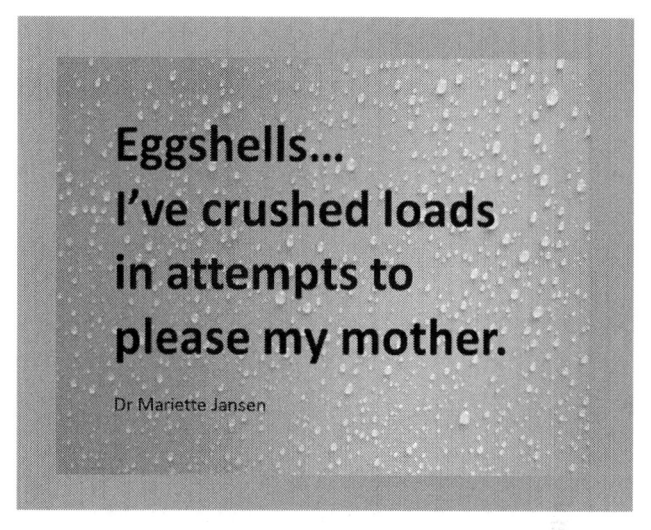

> **Eggshells... I've crushed loads in attempts to please my mother.**
>
> Dr Mariette Jansen

If you want to keep yourself safe and sane in the environment of a narcissist, I suggest you start making changes to your mental attitude, your ways of thinking, how you behave, which actions you take and develop some skills. This is not always easy, as at first this can feel very unnatural and you will not always achieve immediate success, but in the long run, you will become who you want to be: the victor.

2. Stress and anxiety

Being under the influence of a narcissist has affected your mental health. Straight thinking, feeling confident and relaxed are a few things that you might remember from before you had one in your life. Or if you have shaken off your narcissistic parent, you might have discovered these as a new experience.

What is anxiety?

Anxiety can be defined from the perspective of feelings, thoughts and behaviour.

1. Feelings

Anxiety is a natural response to an uncomfortable situation. Everybody experiences anxiety at times. It is an instinctive response to protect us from bad stuff happening to us. An external event triggers the amygdala (stress centre) and the brain produces the stress hormones adrenaline and cortisol so you are ready to fight or flight. When you have been with a narcissist, your system perceives this person as unsafe and the amygdala fires up. Your body will respond with butterflies, sweaty hands and/or heart palpitations.

2. Thoughts

Thoughts are mental reactions to a physical experience. When the body shows signs of anxiety, the mind starts worrying and creates a whirlwind of irrational thoughts, unstoppable and uncontrollable. Those thoughts work like a magnet and attract more and heavier thoughts around worries. It is impossible to step back and examine your thoughts. Confusion is a state of anxiety. Not knowing what is coming, feeling out of control and not understanding what is happening creates anxiety. Narcissists aim is to create confusion and all that goes with it.

3. Behaviour

Humans avoid pain and look for pleasure. Anxiety is uncomfortable and the natural response is to try to avoid or dampen it. That results in giving in or ignoring the cause of anxiety, secretly hoping it will pass. Making excuses so it seems less serious.

Anxiety continues when the situation goes on. In this case, when the narcissist continues to play a role in your life, anxiety is being fed as you are continuously on the lookout for danger (in order to protect yourself) and avoidance strategies actually make it worse.

Successful strategies and therapies to reduce anxiety are based on changing your thoughts, feelings or behaviour. Becoming rational instead of irrational, controlling feelings and applying new behaviour.

When your anxiety is caused by a narcissist, the only thing to aim for is to contain your anxiety by knowing what is going on (stop the confusion), becoming detached and containing feelings, and learning responses that will keep you safe and sane.

As a narcissist instils fear, the anxiety will be there as long as they are around. Accept that and work on managing the anxiety as well as you can.

3. The three key questions

It is difficult to fully understand a narcissist, but it will help to ask the following questions when looking at their actions. It will throw a light on the situation from their perspective and the more you ask these questions, the easier it will get to recognise what is going on. Keep asking these questions in any situations with your narcissist. I will make clear what is going on.

> Whenever you are in a situation with a narcissist, these are the 3 key questions:
>
> 1. How does this affect their safety?
> This is about protecting the fragile ego.
> 2. How does this feed their satisfaction?
> This is about the Narcissistic Supply.
> 3. Whatever they say, how do I know they speak the truth?
> This is about the control and manipulation.
>
> Dr Mariette Jansen

You will be the victor if you step into your power, embrace your freedom and live life your way.

- Respecting yourself and knowing how to look after yourself, so you won't be a target for another narcissist.
- Trusting and having the confidence that you will never find yourself in an unhappy and unsettling situation, where you have been terrorised.
- Recognising the danger signs and knowing how to respond to keep yourself safe.

Breaking free from a narcissist usually comes with a price: you might lose money, possessions, family and friends, but you will gain self-respect, freedom and the opportunity to build a happy life.

This chapter is all about recognising and applying actions to keep yourself in the best place.

Claim your victory

4. Your toolbox

The rest of this chapter is about mental attitudes, actions and behaviours to keep yourself safe and sane. Start applying one or two at the time, until you have mastered them all.

1. Pen and paper

These are the primary tools and your best mates in the process of evolving from victim to victor. What is going on in your head and in your heart, can be very clear to you one day, but the next you might think and feel confused and lost. The power of writing makes thoughts and feelings more tangible and organised.

I suggest you get yourself a lovely notebook and pen and carry it with you. Whenever there is something worthwhile to write down, you have your kit with you.

Alternatively, you can order the workbook From Victim to Victor via Amazon. It offers loads of space for download pages and conscious notes as well as all your notes about your narcissist's traits and other exercises mentioned in this book.

Two ways to use writing: download pages and conscious notes.

1.1. Download Pages: empty your mind onto paper

Downloading pages is a tool to gain clarity without focused thinking. The suggestion is to do this daily for 20 minutes. Just pick up a pen and start writing without lifting your pen off the paper. The unconscious stream that flows forth is of great value in processing life. There are no restrictions on what you can write about. You can use the download pages as a personal journal. You can use them as a means to plan out projects. You can write stories if you like. You can fill the pages with the same word, over and over, if that works for you. Some topics you could try, if you're stuck for ideas, include:

What happened yesterday; what's going to happen today; future plans (of any kind); things you like; things you don't like; hopes; fears; things that make you angry; favourite memories; someone (or something) that you care about. And of course, anything related to your narcissist.

These are just suggestions and they should be treated as starting points because an interesting thing happens over time. As your conscious mind disengages a bit from the process, you may find surprising things appear on the paper. Wants, dreams, fears, old hurts, rants: anything can appear if your subconscious is ready to express. This is a good thing. Don't stop writing, no matter what emerges from the tip of your pen, until you finish your 20 minutes. If some thoughts try to intrude, let them intrude and write them down.

Remember: no one ever needs to read these pages, including you.

Downloading pages is a particularly good tool if you have conscious (or subconscious) worries, psychic wounds, fears, or other concerns that you may be ignoring or suppressing. Bringing them to the surface and getting them down on paper helps reduce anxiety and stops energy from being lost to unproductive thoughts and feelings (a caution: this can be emotionally draining).

Writing down your thoughts as they appear can help to lift their burden from your mind. This is a way of de-cluttering. You are tidying up your mental desk so that you can do more important work.

Let your thoughts speak for themselves.

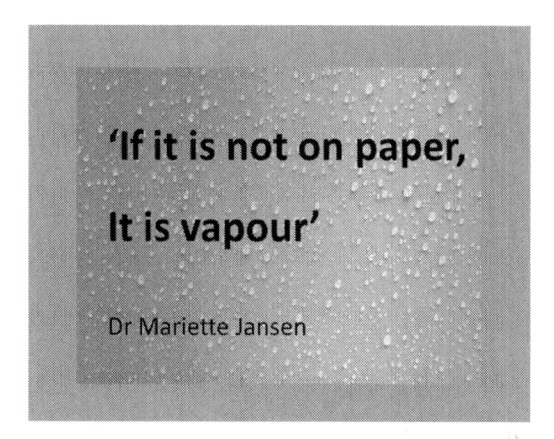

> **'If it is not on paper,**
>
> **It is vapour'**
>
> Dr Mariette Jansen

Some therapists believe that this type of exercise should be done as quickly as possible. You should write as fast as you possibly can, even if it means that your pages look like hen scratchings. The theory behind this is that when you are writing faster than your conscious mind can think, you are tapping directly into the subconscious and bringing your true feelings to the surface.

You don't have to be a speed demon when writing your download pages, but it's another variation that could be useful to you.

To discover what it will do for you, just pick up a pen, get a piece of paper and write regularly for several weeks and see what comes out of it.

One of my clients calls this process 'dust writing'. She refers to it as dusting her brain of all the doubt and noise and as a result she gets a clearer picture.

Happy writing!

1.2. Conscious notes: write down events, evidence, thoughts and epiphanies

Collecting information serves a range of purposes.

- **a.** It is easy to forget specific details, but writing them down will jog your memory.
- **b.** When you are being manipulated, your version of events might be denied and you might start doubting yourself. Not so, if it is all written down.
- **c.** Giving you a clear understanding of what is actually happening through the recording of events.
- **d.** Collecting evidence

2. Fluffing up

To keep the peace and give yourself a break from the pressure of a narcissist, fluff them up. It is not a long-term solution, but it offers respite. A narcissist needs the stroke, the admiration and to feel important: the Narcissistic Supply. If you give it to them because you have an ulterior motive of wanting something from them, this often works.

The mum who wants the narcissistic dad to help with bathing the kids will get him to do the job by fluffing him up. 'I know you are so good at this. And even though I know you are tired and I am asking a lot, but could you please be a super daddy and help out?'

3. Gray rocking

Gray rocking is a mental attitude where you behave completely detached. You don't absorb anything and also don't give anything out. You become the most boring person imaginable. You have nothing important or interesting to talk about, nothing to share and you don't engage in drama or confusion. Find safe topics to talk about with your narcissist, which are of no interest to you, but may be to them, so they can chat away. Or find a topic they are not interested in so they will switch off.

It requires alertness to behave like this, especially if your narcissist tries to push your buttons, but training leads to mastery.

4. Refrain from giving personal information

Personal data is stored in the mind of a narcissist to be used when it is convenient and useful to them. Their memory is amasing and they retain all information you offer them and details about events for decades. This also relates to opinions and ideas. Don't share those either. The more they know, the more vulnerable you become. They will use your 'data' in situations where they can insult you and humiliate you within a group of others.

Do talk about what you have established as 'safe' topics. The latest fashion, football, movies, anything with a sense of normality that lacks personal elements.

5. Find the narcissistic reason for compliments and kind words

Are they really compliments? Are those words really kind? Always ask yourself what your narcissist wants to achieve for themselves. It is never about you. Everything they say serves them. Keep that in mind. How about the husband who only gives a compliment because he wants sex?

What is the aim of my narcissist here? Ask the same 3 questions again to find out more.

> Whenever you are in a situation with a narcissist, these are the 3 key questions:
>
> 1. How does this affect their safety?
> This is about protecting the fragile ego.
> 2. How does this feed their satisfaction?
> This is about the Narcissistic Supply.
> 3. Whatever they say, how do I know they speak the truth?
> This is about the control and manipulation.
>
> Dr Mariette Jansen

6. Mind the law

Be aware that narcissists are above the law and have been found in situations where they were fraudulent. This can impact you and you should always check legal papers, insurances and liabilities. If your romantic or business partner makes the decisions, insist to know what they are about and be very alert and careful. Always check and double-check, ideally with a third party.

7. Don't feed their envy

Envy and jealousy can have two forms for a narcissist. They either want to outperform you or take away what you have. If you have or do something that makes them jealous, they will spoil your joy. Keep yourself safe by not communicating about it.

Claim your victory

8. You can't help or rescue them

Narcissists will not change, because they don't want to. They are in the best place they can be. They are convinced they don't need to change as they are perfect. Some people I spoke with wanted to help their narcissist to become a better parent, a nicer partner, a more sociable person. They felt they couldn't let them ruin their lives… Yet they didn't see (at that point in time) that their own lives were ruined. A narcissist doesn't want to be rescued. They are in the best place ever. They are happy in their unhappiness. There might be situations where you feel sorry for them, but remember that you have feelings, they don't. Apart from fear, anger and hate.

9. Give up hope

Narcissists pretend to understand and change if it opens the door to more Narcissistic Supply. But it is all fake. Don't believe and hope that things can change for the better. It is part of their strategy of creating confusion. Lots of victims swing from fear, to hope and back to fear. But the spiral is always downwards. In all the interviews I have held, the pretended change was short-lived and afterwards, life always became worse.

> **'I thought he couldn't help he had a rough childhood.**
>
> **No warmth, no love, no appreciation.**
> **No wonder he was so manipulative and keen to get what he wanted. Not considering others.**
> **Focus on self.**
>
> **I thought I was the one who could rescue him. Teach him how it is to be loved, teach him to love me back.**
>
> **It took me 30 years to admit he was beyond rescuing. And then it was me who needed to be rescued.'**
>
> A survivor of a narcissistic relationship

Imagine you are walking in a park. You see a dog. The dog looks at you with pretty eyes, tilts his head as if to ask for a stroke and you bend down to stroke him. After two strokes, the dog opens his mouth and bites you.

That hurts! You might even develop septicaemia.

You go home to look after yourself. The next day you walk in the park. The same dog comes up to you. Now you have been warned and you keep a distance. But the dog twists his tale and seems to be so enthusiastic that you think the event from yesterday was very unnatural for him. Maybe he wasn't well or had a real off day. You pick up his ball and just as you are about to throw it, he jumps up and bites you again.

It's even worse than yesterday's bite.

What do you think you will do the next time you meet this same dog?

Be nice, so he can bite you again? Or keep a distance to keep yourself safe?

10. Never trust their actions and words

A narcissist will always act to get what they want. Even if their words seem kind, the kindness is towards themselves. When they seem to want to help, watch out. They want to confuse you in order to be in control. Manipulation is their primary language and they use it to confuse you. When you are confused, it is easy to brainwash you, undermine your confidence and remove you from yourself. A lost soul is the easiest target. They never act with honesty and decency and you never take what they say at face value.

What is behind their words and actions?

Ask the three questions.

11. You won't be able to understand them, don't even try

A narcissist's internal world is so different from people who feel and are empathic, that you will never be able to understand them. They have a way of getting under your skin and sneaking into your mind. How much energy have you spent so far on them? Trying to make sense of their behaviour, thinking of new strategies to help them or finding a solution, working out how you can get closer?

You will never find the answers. They will continue to surprise you. Unpleasantly. By their actions and conversations. The number of times that I was gobsmacked at my mother's reaction is uncountable. You are living in a different world. Stay in yours, and let them carry on in theirs. By now you will know more about narcissists and their way of thinking and acting, but you don't really understand. And you don't have to. You just need to be alert.

> When I was a little girl, I often wondered why me and my mother always thought differently.
>
> I thought I was kind, she told me I was selfish.
> I tried to help out, she said I didn't do enough.
> I told a true story, she called me hysterical.
> If only I knew then,
> What I know now,
>
> It wasn't me who got it wrong.
>
> Dr Mariette Jansen

12. Flying monkeys alert

Narcissists recruit their allies to create an army of Flying Monkeys. They are there to serve your narcissist. They might do some dirty work, via emails, texts or conversations so your narcissist still has a clean sheet. Monkeys are often recruited through the role of 'the victim' and a 'smear campaign' about you. People feel sorry for the narcissist and want to help the narcissist. They feel anger and disgust towards you, based on the information the narcissist has provided. Monkeys are either weak, they don't see through the manipulation; or nastiness, they love to be part of something ugly. If you used to have an open relationship with one of those monkeys, you could try to talk to them. Your narcissist will have chosen them wisely and the chances are small that you will be seen for who you really are. You have lost those people. Take your loss and move on.

Flying monkeys are an extension of your narcissist and they will report back everything you say to them. Choose your words wisely and even better, detach from them and ignore them.

13. Gaslighting antidotes

Gaslighting is a tactic when someone is manipulated to doubt their own reality and think they are going mad. It creates a psychological horror story inside someone's head. It is a form of mental and emotional abuse, which is often seen in narcissists and sociopaths. Victims of gaslighting start to doubt their reality and sanity, because they are told again and again that they got it wrong, talk nonsense and recall situations that haven't taken place or took place in a very different way. Gaslighting victims think they are going mad.

The name originates from a 1944 movie entitled *Gaslight*, in which a manipulative husband tries to make his wife think she is losing her mind by making subtle changes in her environment, including slowly and steadily dimming the flame of a gas lamp. He also abuses and controls her, alienates her from family and friends and she loses all sense of what is true and what isn't, feeling she is going crazy.

Signals that you are being gaslighted are:

Being lied to – gaslighters lie convincingly and even with evidence of their deception; they will not give in. The result is that you start to doubt your version of events.

Example: you have been asked to book a table for dinner on Friday at 7 pm. On Friday, you get dressed and are ready to go at 6.30, only to be asked where you are going. When you mention their request for a reservation you are met with denial. 'Where did that idea come from?'

Being discredited – gaslighters spread rumours and gossip about you. Example: they may pretend they are worried about the recent changes in your behaviour, your instability and weird reactions. They are concerned as this might be the first signals of your historic mental health issue returning (which is a lie). What will happen if you start to confide in people about the negatives of your relationship? This is all part of the alienation process where you lose people and your narcissist gets allies instead.

Thoughts and feelings are dismissed – whatever you say is dismissed. The gaslighter will call you hysterical, over-sensitive, overreacting, even psychotic, unreasonable and the like. Whatever you say, you can't be taken seriously. You will never be validated.

Example: if you tell your narcissist you are upset about the dinner date; you would be told to not go over the top and get over it.

Shifting blame – the gaslighter will twist a situation in such a way that you are the one to blame. If you didn't behave the way you did, they wouldn't have to treat you the way they do.

Example: if you were not making a fuss about your mistakes all the time, they would have taken you out to dinner.

Compassionate words – using kind and loving language to manipulate you. 'I love you so much, how can you think I would hurt you?'

Example: 'I would never put you down for making a mistake about that Friday dinner.'

Gaslighting is subtle and it usually takes time to discover that you are being manipulated. Signals that indicate you are being gaslighted are changes in your mental state.

The checklist below will give you an indication of how much you are affected by gaslighting.

Uncertain about your feelings and your view of the world	
Feeling insecure	
Doubting your judgement	
Afraid of speaking up or voicing an opinion	
Worried you will do the wrong thing	
Walking on eggshells	
Feeling powerless	
Feeling alone	
Worried that people will think you are strange, crazy or unstable, just as you have been told by your gaslighter	
Feeling strange, crazy and unstable	
Wondering where your strength and confidence has gone	
Feeling confused	
Worried about making decisions	
Apologising a lot	
Feeling inadequate	
Not recognising yourself anymore	

Examples

As long as she can remember, Elsie has been told by her mother what to feel. She fell on her knee one day and told her mum she was angry because one of the boys in school had tripped her up. Her mother immediately told her that she wasn't angry. Her knee hurt and that is what she felt. Elsie thought to herself that she hardly felt the pain, but was absolutely livid with the boy who tripped her. Every time Elsie voiced her feelings, her mother kept on correcting her. The outcome was that Elsie lived with a lot of confusion as she knew what she felt inside, but it wasn't acknowledged as the 'right thing' and she doubted what was hers and what wasn't.

A narcissistic mum Emily and her daughter Ilse had been shopping a few weeks earlier. Emily bought a blue top, which would go with a specific skirt she has. When Ilse asked about the blue top, the mother said: 'What blue top? I would never buy blue. I just don't like it.' The daughter would recall the situation, reminding her of the shop and what the sales assistant said about the top, but the mother would say to her daughter she got it totally wrong, adding 'your memory has always been bad.'

Sally told her husband he had disturbed her sleep when he came home very late the evening before. He completely ignored her remark but mentioned how she had been complaining about sleeping badly for years now and how she was always restless and kept him awake more often than not. Sally is convinced she is a good sleeper… or maybe not?

After an evening out, Albert accuses his narcissistic girlfriend Vicky of flirting with one of his mates. It has happened before but she turns to him and says: 'Darling, I love you. I would never do something like that. And if you hadn't been drinking and had paid me more attention, then I would not have had to talk to others, would I? By the way, your friends were saying you've been behaving a bit strange lately anyway. Not the fun person you used to be…'

One incident where you are being told you are wrong when you know you are right doesn't make it gaslighting. When it happens regularly and convincingly with effects as listed in the checklist, then it is gaslighting.

How to counteract gaslighting?

Start recording events

Like Ilse, who went shopping with her mum. If she had noted down what had been said and what had been bought, she wouldn't doubt her recall of the events and therefore start to question her own judgment (and ultimately, her sanity).

Take photos as supporting evidence

This evidence is not for you to share with your narcissist, it is for you to know that you got it right. Regardless of what someone else has said to you.

Talk to a trusted friend

Pick a friend who isn't totally wrapped up by your narcissist. Sometimes friends only see the pleasant presentation and can't imagine how someone can behave very differently at home. If you don't want to talk to a friend, maybe look for a coach or a therapist.

14. Stop eating carrots – push and pull

One way of controlling a rabbit is by dangling a carrot in front of it and then taking it away. Or maybe give it time to take a bite of it. It will keep the rabbit eager and interested. And it will keep the carrot dangler in control.

A victim of a narcissistic abuser longs for love, connection and a 'normal' relationship. The carrot, in this case, is a response that makes the victim think that things are changing. Yes, I am understood. Yes, I am loved. I got it wrong. As long as there is hope for improvement from the side of the victim, the narcissist has the power. And therefore, they need the hope to continue. This push and pull behaviour is typical for the narcissist.

Dr Daniel Fox defined a three-step relationship cycle, which entails glorifying, belittling and abandoning. It is particularly clear in a romantic relationship, but is also applied in family and friendship relations.

Glorifying

Glorifying happens at the start of a new romantic relationship: you're having a great time, there is fun, you receive a lot of attention, you feel adored and everything is wonderful. Your narcissist will tell you that 'you are the one' and that they have never felt so close to anyone else. Really special.

In a parent-child relationship, the narcissist suddenly treats you as the golden child. You can't do anything wrong and it might even feel like you are loved.

Belittling

This phase is followed by belittling. There are some critical comments about your appearance, the way you do things, what you say, what you do. At first, these comments are quite subtle and as the memory of the glorifying time is still fresh, the tendency is to not really take these comments too seriously. However, the criticism develops into stronger comments and starts to involve a broader area, such as family, friends. This affects your self-worth and it becomes more hurtful. This is when the doubt starts to crop up. Where does this feeling of unhappiness come from? Narcissists are very good at reading their partners and undermining their confidence, before they enter the next phase of abandoning.

Abandoning

This is the phase of fear and the 'who do you think you are?' Especially, 'who do you think you are without me? I am putting up with you, but nobody else would. Even though you are no great shakes, I am loyal to you and I will stay with you and support you if you do as I say. Otherwise, I need to give up on you.'

It is a psychological reversal process, where the partner or child is made to feel anxious about losing the narcissist. At this stage, they will show glorifying behaviour again, which will bring the hope back that everything will be fine.

And so, the cycle continues. The cycle can take minutes, it can take days. It is a very effective capturing strategy.

> He looked at me
> As if I disgusted him
> Then he spat
> I will break you
> His eyes fired up
> You will crawl for me
> And regret you ever tried to stand up to me.
>
> Dr Mariette Jansen

How to deal with the push and pull?

Observe different situations without judgment. Describe and be factual.

Make detailed notes on dialogues and interactions.

Mark each situation as either glorifying, belittling or abandoning.

Mark each event with a happiness score between 0 – 10.

Is there a pattern?

How do you respond to each situation? Are you defensive, aggressive, lost, desperate, hopeless?

Before you can take the next steps, you need to have a clear picture of the details.

Can you respond differently on the inside? Instead of being upset, can you stay detached? Experiment with different responses to find out what works best for you.

15. Stick to your frame

The meaning you give to situations depends upon your point of view. When you reframe, you choose a different point of view. The best example is the consideration of whether a glass is half full or half empty. One is from a positive perspective, the other from a negative.

Reframing is a well-known technique in certain psychotherapies and it is helpful when you want to change negative thoughts or events into more positive or constructive ones.

> "If a problem can't be solved within the frame it was conceived, the solution lies in reframing the problem."
>
> *Brian McGreevy (screenwriter)*

Reframing is used by a narcissist to shine an unexpected light on a situation. It is not one that is in favour of other people. They reframe to get confirmation of what is important to them. Often the reframing is putting someone down, undermining them or glorifying themselves.

Example

The daughter, who was in her thirties, left her three children and husband over the Easter weekend, travelled for eight hours to visit her dad in hospital, stayed over, then travelled back the next day. She executed an act of kindness and love towards her father. Her original plans were jeopardised and the weekend for her whole family turned out very differently. Not much fun, with mum missing. The daughter was also very disappointed to miss out on their Easter weekend, but life got in the way. When she was about to leave to travel back home again, her narcissistic mother reframed the situation, from a kind and loving gesture to 'Well, you got a nice weekend away from your family and got some personal time in. That was nice for you'. As if it had been a joyful experience. The mother reframed the kind act into a selfish act. Otherwise the daughter would get praise and might outshine the mother.

Usually reframing comes as a surprise as the narcissistic way of thinking is quite alien to that of a non-narcissist. Being on the receiving end of reframing can be very unsettling. This surprise, and feeling unsettled, can leave a victim lost for words and worse, lost to rational thinking. Instead, it is easy to become overwhelmed with a negative feeling about oneself.

I remember that I was often told I was a very bad person, but I couldn't get my head around it as I knew I was coming from a place of love. I didn't mean any harm, but by reframing, my mother managed to make me think of my actions as selfish ones instead of kind ones.

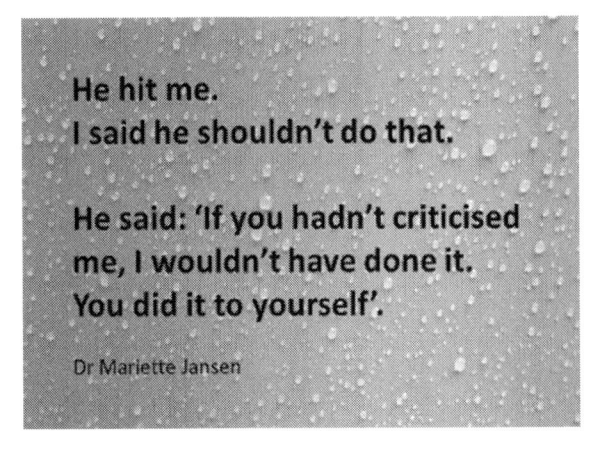

> **He hit me.**
> **I said he shouldn't do that.**
>
> **He said: 'If you hadn't criticised me, I wouldn't have done it. You did it to yourself'.**
>
> Dr Mariette Jansen

How to deal with reframing?

Recognise the reframing for what it is. Just another point of view. Remember that everyone is entitled to their opinion, but it doesn't mean that the narcissist's one is the right one.

Make sure you are clear about your frame and hang on to that. You don't need to discuss it with the narcissist; if possible, just ignore it and shake it off. If that is not possible, acknowledge their point of view as interesting but stick to yours.

Then ask the 3 key questions.

16. Find a response to memories

Narcissists have the memory of an elephant. They store information about you in their head and bring it out whenever it is convenient for them.

When you meet a narcissist for the first time, they come across as if they are really interested in you. They ask loads of questions and the conversation revolves around you. Most likely, you will find it easy to talk to them and might reveal more personal information than you usually would.

The narcissist will absorb it all and will get back to you at a time when they can hit you with it or use it to their advantage. They will use any information about you that could harm you and therefore make them feel better. They feed off exploiting others and feeling stronger and more in control.

Examples: 'Well, you are not very trustworthy as you told me you did steal a scarf from M&S.' This had been told to them as an anecdote about coincidentally discovering a scarf amongst your shopping. The memory has been reframed and then thrown back at you.

My mother delighted in shouting at me: 'You were the one who cancelled the agency.' Leaving me for a few seconds to wonder what the heck she was talking about… It was an attempt when I was around 27 to go for family therapy. I had made all the arrangements but as I had just started individual therapy, I decided it would cost too much. I cancelled for good reasons. This happened over 30 years ago. Only because she mentioned it, am I able to recall that situation. For her though, it is on the list of my 'wrong-doings', ready to be presented at the right time.

Whatever you once said or did, will stay with them as if it is written in stone. It is impossible for a narcissist to be fluid and reconsider something which took place some time ago could have changed. They are very rigid and unable to put things in a new perspective.

How to deal with their ability to remember

Don't give them any ammunition. Try to keep communication to a minimum. Don't offer personal information, thoughts, feelings, anything. It will be used against you in a direct attack or via indirect bad-mouthing.

If you are attacked with information, put it in perspective and let it go if you can. Alternatively, laugh it off and tell them you have changed. 'That was then, this is now.'

17. Dismantle, divide and rule

'Divide and rule', also known as 'divide and conquer', is an efficient way to avoid power clusters and make sure you are in control.

It is a well-known strategy applied by Julius Caesar, Napoleon and others to gain and maintain power. Avoiding the formation of groups or breaking up existing ones, it makes it easier to control and dominate.

Narcissists are brilliant at this.

Claim your victory

A good tool for divide and rule is to create gossipy stories and play people off against each other. The stories are often not true.

'Did you know that Ann got really upset by Bea, who didn't keep her promise and Ann felt very let down. I don't think Bea is very trustworthy. I would be careful with her if I were you. Just saying, just warning you.' This is a made-up story aimed to put Bea in a bad light and drive a wedge between Ann and Bea.

'Don't invite Pat to that evening out because she has financial problems as she has lost her job.' The narcissist suggests that Pat has lost her job, which isn't true, making sure Pat is then excluded from an evening out with like-minded people who might gang up against the narcissist. Pat would be upset by being left out and it could create a lot of drama and confusion within the friendship group.

Blatant lying is never a problem for narcissists. My mother did a very effective 'divide and rule' when I visited my parents. My parents, sister and brother all lived in a small town in The Netherlands. I wanted to see my sister, who had just moved into a new home. When I made tracks to go, my mother told me she wasn't around that weekend. So, I didn't go.

I didn't hear from my sister for two months. She didn't answer texts or voicemails but eventually, we spoke and I discovered that my mother lied to me when I visited. My sister had been home, decorating her new house and waiting for my visit. When I didn't turn up, she was massively disappointed and angry and didn't want to be in touch with me. This, of course, suited my mother to the bone: no contact, no power cluster.

Another variation of 'divide and rule' is triangulation. This is an indirect technique where one person acts as a messenger between two others. Examples are speaking on behalf of others, 'Your father said this about you' and 'Your friend was hoping you had done more than you have'. It is brilliant if you want to create upset, misunderstandings between people and drama without lying. It is all about twisting facts and narcissists thrive on it.

How to deal with divide and rule

Never believe a narcissist. If other people are involved, always check the stories with them. If you receive advice from a narcissist, always check it out.

Always, and this is a very helpful attitude in all areas of life, only speak for yourself and not for or about others. This is the only way to be in control and know what is going on for yourself. If other people make up stories and situations, it's up to them. This way you will never get involved.

18. You are good enough

Most victims have believed, and some still do sometimes, that they are never good enough. The continuous exposure to put-downs results in that belief. That isn't true. 'You are good enough' and a big part of your recovery revolves around this.

> **REMEMBER**
> **It is not you**
> **You are not at fault**
> **You haven't done anything wrong**
> **You don't have to apologise**
> **You shouldn't doubt yourself**
> **You should trust yourself**
> **Acknowledge your loving nature**
> **Your positive intentions**
> **You are the victim of a NARCISSIST**
>
> Dr Mariette Jansen

Claim your victory

A put-down is a way of insulting someone, ridiculing them and making them feel less of themselves. They are subtle with a sting, such as a back-handed compliment or criticism disguised as a joke.

The most effective put-downs are those that are not in your face and lend themselves to multiple interpretations. The sting could be in the tone of voice, the presentation of the content or just referring to a very personal situation. It is impossible to criticise the remark as the literal content is not a clear put-down and if the narcissist is challenged, they will point out that you are too sensitive or hysterical.

Questions

How about the question: 'Do you like that colour?' about your t-shirt. The tone of voice and facial expression carry the critical content, but strictly speaking, it is just a question.

Passive-aggressive remarks

How about a passive-aggressive remark? I was upset when the handle of my favourite handbag broke. My friend commented: 'Well, it was only a cheap bag'. In other words, it is not worth being upset about something as cheap as your handbag.

After the announcement of a pregnancy, the phone rings and the narcissist says: 'I don't know what you were thinking, but I guess I have to congratulate you.' The remark implies the woman is crazy to have become pregnant.

General but personal statements

General statements that are meant personally, such as 'There are people around who never seem to be able to make the right decisions.' What actually is being said is that the person they are talking about isn't able to make the right decisions.

Personal revelation

In a group of his friends, the girlfriend says: 'You mean, he is not moody with you guys? Well, you should see him at home!'

Recalling a memory

The slim wife says to the voluptuous sister-in-law: 'Oh, I was filled with disgust when I first saw you. You were so fat, absolutely disgraceful.' That is not a memory that is worth sharing. It is only meant to be hurtful and put someone down.

Interfering with personal choices

Narcissists easily overstep boundaries with comments about someone's personal decision. 'I don't think you should take that route to work; it's clear you have no sense of direction.'

Devaluing a positive action

The husband bought his wife a beautiful bunch of flowers. She took a photo and sent it to her family's WhatsApp group. The narcissistic brother replied: 'Tesco?'

And so, it goes on and on.

Recognising a put-down requires the victim to step into the mindset of the narcissist and analyse a remark from the perspective of how it could be hurtful, humiliating or disrespectful.

Most victims of a narcissist are empathic and positive and it will take some time to process a remark as a critical comment. When you are on the receiving end of those put-downs, over time your empathy and positivity will reduce and even disappear to be replaced by hurt, lost confidence and fear.

How to deal with put-downs

Write down each potential put-down remark you've heard.

Consider the put down with the following questions:

- Is it kind?
- Is it respectful?
- Is it helpful?
- Is it true for you?
- If it isn't true, then write down what is true and embrace that.

19. Use the JADE technique

When people are insecure, they usually present their choices and decisions with a lot of background information: a detailed explanation, some extra information, pros and cons, the thinking process and more irrelevant details.

In a relationship with a narcissist, you will be the one who is insecure and possibly fearful when talking about one of your decisions.

Do you often find yourself waffling on about a decision or choice you have made?

That is due to the fear that your narcissist might reject your choice or challenge you.

But is it relevant?

If you made a decision and you are sure about it, is there any need to defend yourself?

You think that providing all that extra detailed justification will help you to feel more secure about it. Actually, it suggests that you are not sure about your decision and that you are absolutely scared to death that someone will stand up against it. You have just given them all the ammunition they need to challenge you.

Your decision, your choice.

You don't owe anyone a reason for your choices. No one has the right to challenge you if you don't want to be challenged.

The way to prevent the challenge is JADE, which is one of the best tools to communicate clearly without fear or doubt.

JADE stands for DO NOT
- *Justify*
- *Argue*
- *Defend*
- *Explain*

The narcissist is always looking to undermine you and will use the information in your justification, defence or explanation to start challenging your decision. You make it easy for them to start an argument, using your own words.

To avoid these situations, apply JADE whenever you can.

20. Ditch the guilt card

Your narcissist will point out at every possible occasion that you have done something wrong. As a result, you might feel guilty about almost everything. But… is it justified?

You can recognise healthy guilt by answering the following three questions:

Is it your responsibility?

If you are responsible for a situation, guilt might be appropriate. Often narcissists will make you responsible for situations, like blaming you when something goes wrong for them. Is it your responsibility that your narcissist is late? Or broke an ankle? Or feels tired? Check the context and if you are not responsible, don't feel guilty.

Did you do something wrong?

The emotion of guilt is healthy if it is about something you did wrong. It is an alarm button and in normal situations will encourage you to make it better again. When your narcissist points the finger, you should check and ask yourself, 'Did I really do something wrong?' If not, then it is a sign to let go of the guilt.

Is this about my truth or someone else's?

Being susceptible to guilt is often rooted in ideas that you grew up with. Along the lines of saying to you as a child, 'If you really love me, you wouldn't be naughty' to a child. 'You should always put others first', 'A good parent controls their child', and more. If you have a narcissistic parent, you will have loads of these ideas. If you have a narcissistic partner, they will continuously throw these types of statements at you.

Examples are: 'If you really love me, you would do this for me' or 'You always want to do your own thing.' Narcissists are very good at playing the guilt card. As they believe are never wrong, they must point the finger at someone else. At you. They will do it in a way that will make you feel really bad about yourself. Any time you feel guilt, ask yourself the three questions above and then decide if it is reasonable to feel guilty.

Part VI:
Summary

> **I owe myself the biggest apology for putting up with what I didn't deserve.**
>
> Dr Mariette Jansen

Having read this book, you should now be able to quickly identify a narcissist and narcissistic traits. Keep in mind that narcissism is a sliding scale and your narcissist might show traits in just one or two categories. Having knowledge about them means you are better equipped to respond to their actions and not be battered by their tricks.

If you are not sure if you have a narcissist in your life, go through the checklist and answer the questions for each box you ticked:

a. How does this affect my happiness? (0-10)

   0 = it doesn't contribute to my happiness at all
   10 = it makes me very happy

b. How does this affect my stress levels? (0-10)

   0 = it doesn't give me any stress
   10 = it completely stresses me out

c. How strongly am I in control? (0-10)

   0 = I am not in control at all
   10 = I feel totally in control

d. How do I react to this situation/trait?

   - What do I feel?
   - What do I think?
   - How do I behave?
   - How do I behave?

Helpful actions

1. Writing and reflecting (download pages and conscious notes)
2. Fluffing up your narcissist if you need a breather
3. Gray rocking and staying detached
4. Establishing topics to talk about (and the 'no go' subjects)
5. Asking the three key questions
6. Dismantling gaslighting
7. Finding patterns through observations and making notes
8. Always checking out what they tell you
9. Applying JADE

Summary

Important to remember

1. Stay away from your narcissist, run as fast as you can.
2. It is not your fault. What has happened to you is not your fault. Your narcissist wants you to believe it is, but if you are their victim, it is because you are empathic and kind. They are cold manipulators.
3. Trust your gut feeling – if it doesn't feel right, it isn't right.
4. You can never trust a narcissist.
5. Withhold personal information.
6. Don't feed their envy.
7. You can't help or rescue them.
8. Mind the law.
9. Give up hope.
10. You are good enough, and a very beautiful, special and valuable person.

Epilogue

This book is my life's work. It sounds pretty dramatic and that is exactly what it is. It gives meaning to my trauma and my suffering. If it turns out that sharing my experiences and knowledge is helping others, then it has all made sense.

Since I started standing up at networking events, presenting myself and my life coaching business with the sentence: 'My mother is a nasty piece of work', the clients streamed in. All were connected to a narcissist – a parent, a partner, an ex-partner, a friend, and all have been very strongly affected by it.

Helping them to see what is going on underneath the surface gives me great satisfaction, because when you have knowledge, you have the option to make choices and decisions. Instead of feeling powerless, you can step into your power and stand up for yourself. If this work has contributed to that process, I have done my job.

What's next?

You have started your journey to move away from your narcissist. To learn to deal with situations and stay in control. To leave the trauma and start your recovery.

It is a huge challenge and there is no need to do it all by yourself.

- Find a coach or counsellor who is a specialist in this area and can support you.
- Join my Facebook group: Narcissism, from victim to surviving to thriving

- Book a free coaching call with me to get advice on your next step: https://mariettejansencoaching.youcanbook.me/

You are not alone and you don't have to make the journey all by yourself.

All my love,

Mariette

If you enjoyed this book, please leave a review on Amazon. It will make it easier to find for people who would benefit.

About the Author

Mariette Jansen is a life coach, psychotherapist, meditation teacher, blogger and speaker.

Mariette obtained a PhD in Communication Science in The Netherlands and worked in corporate organisations. An opportunity to retrain arose after the birth of her eldest son, when she qualified as a psychotherapist, a counselling tutor and a meditation teacher. After ten years, she decided to focus her client work more on action and goals and has worked since 2011 as a successful life coach.

Mariette always knew that something was wrong, but couldn't find what it was. Her parents kept on telling her she was the one who was wrong. But, Mariette knew it couldn't be just her.

Growing up in a dysfunctional family took its toll. One of Mariette reactions to her situation was to develop an eating disorder, Bulimia Nervosa, which lasted 22 years.

Although Mariette now realises that she grew up in a narcissistic family she only started to understand the full extent of her situation in her late 50's. Her mother, her main narcissist, was the most important person in her life and most of her actions were inspired by the wish to please her and be on the receiving end of love, acceptance and respect. It never happened.

As a result of her own realisation, Mariette discovered narcissism and how it plays out. It was an eye-opener and a sanity-saver.

All of a sudden, clarity hit and life made sense. It got easier to understand how to deal with it all and apply the behaviours that would support her on-going happiness and well-being.

She met the love of her life, Iain, when she was 37 and moved to the UK to be with him. She never wanted children, but being with Iain pushed the maternal button and at the age of 40 their first child was born, followed 2.5 years later by their second. Both boys, which was a relief.

More and more victims of narcissistic abuse have found their way to her practice, thanks to recommendations, Facebook posts (drdestresstips), her Facebook group (groups/movingawayfromnarcissism/) and her talks.

If this book has helped you in any way, please post a review on Amazon. It will make it easier for others to find it and get the support they are looking for.

Thank you.

Bibliography and references

Books

Arabi, Shadhida (2017). Power, Surviving and thriving after narcissistic abuse. Brooklyn: Thought Catalog Books.

Bradshaw, John (1933). The Family, A new way of creating solid self-esteem. Florida: Health Communications Inc.

Hatfield, E., Cacioppo, J. T. and Rapson, R. L. (1994). *Emotional contagion.* Cambridge: Cambridge University Press.

Jackson, Theresa (2017). How to handle a narcissist. Indie publishers.

Marsh, Abigail (2017). The **Fear** Factor: How One Emotion Connects Altruists, Psychopaths, and Everyone In-Between. New York: Basic books.

Stewart, Ian & Joines, Vann (1987). TA Today, A New Introduction to Transactional Analysis. Nottingham: Lifespace Publishing.

Web links

https://www.drsyrasderksen.com/blog/seeing-narcissism-in-the-brain

https://psychcentral.com/blog/new-research-may-support-the-existence-of-empaths/

https://www.lifeadvancer.com/empaths-and-narcissists-attraction/

https://healingtreenonprofit.org/wp-content/uploads/2016/01/Trauma-Bonds-by-Patrick-Carnes-1.pdf

https://cptsdfoundation.org/2019/11/22/recognising-and-breaking-a-trauma-bond/

https://youtu.be/Y1OGSeKsMlo – Daniel Fox about the 3 parts in the narcissistic relationship

Printed in Poland
by Amazon Fulfillment
Poland Sp. z o.o., Wrocław